SIN
CITY

**CRIME AND
CORRUPTION IN
20TH-CENTURY
SYDNEY**

TIM GIRLING-BUTCHER

Foreword by the Hon Michael Kirby

HISTORIC HOUSES TRUST

FOREWORD THE HON MICHAEL KIRBY AC CMG

From its convict origins, Sydney had its fair share of the seven deadly sins. *Anger* in abundance, as those transported came to terms with their isolation and military rule. *Avarice*, as the colony evolved from subsistence to respectability. *Envy*, as the descendants of the troopers tried fruitlessly to suppress the more talented children of the convicts. *Gluttony* in the eating houses that sprang up everywhere. *Lechery* and *lust* in the brothels, streets and dance halls, where sex was openly sold. *Pride* amongst the bunyip aristocracy and the local 'establishment' that mimicked the manners of the gentry back 'home'. And *sloth* on the beaches and mountains where it was so easy to just do nothing in the sunshine.

So Sydney had all of these 'sins'. It still has. Collecting great numbers of immigrants in a bustling port town around a harbour playground made it inevitable that fallible humans would indulge in a 'sin' or two. People cannot live in a playground without wanting to play. For most, that is just human nature.

The problem for Sydney was that its rulers espoused a stern protestant view of the seven dastardly inclinations, considering that indulgence in them would lead to eternal damnation. Saving weak mortals from their inclinations in that respect (even if the 'sins' hurt no-one but themselves) became a purpose of law and order.

Alcohol and drugs were wicked because they tended to promote sloth. So did gluttony. The Empire was built upon furious energy. Lechery and lust were no good because they encouraged extra-marital relations. Moreover, they tended to lead to anger or sloth. Gambling was intolerable because it grew out of avarice and envy. Sloth, you see, was at the heart of them all. Distractions from the work ethic were to be strongly discouraged.

The fundamental problem with this thesis about life was that the overwhelming majority of Sydneysiders did not believe it or could not live up to its expectations.

They just wanted to have a good time. And this meant indulging in drinking or other drugs, gambling and sex. Between the 'standards' dictated by the law and the ardent desires of much of the population opened up a gulf demanding services. The provision of those services promised big money.

In this outpost of Empire, trying to enforce the morality of 'home' became the duty of judges, prosecutors and police. But some of these guardians of 'morality' inevitably themselves fell victim to the temptation of the 'sins'. Or they found that there was money to be had (often in great quantities) by turning a blind eye to the 'sinners'. They could salve their consciences by assuring themselves that 'sin' would go on happening whatever they did; that laws would not be changed because of hypocritical officials, often themselves sinners; and that a little money between friends would harm no-one.

Look at the stories of the characters collected in this book. Some, it is true, were nasty, violent people. But if you dig deeply enough, you will find that most of them would probably have been kind to children and animals and slept peacefully at night, believing that they were doing little more than serving the insatiable demands of their fellow citizens.

I knew Murray Farquhar, one time Chief Magistrate of New South Wales, when I was Chairman of the Australian Law Reform Commission in the 1970s. He was a delightful man, well ahead of his time in embracing the newfangled theories of criminology and penology. He exuded sympathy for the prisoners he had to punish, sometimes for victimless crimes that he probably regarded with disdain. He was ever supportive of reform and innovation. But he was found to be corrupt. That was a shocking discovery for the judiciary and legal profession. At the heart of his guilt lay gambling, as it did with many of the others on our list. Neddy Smith appeared before me in the Court of Appeal in connection with a charge of contempt of court for refusing to answer perfectly reasonable questions. The court imposed a whopping fine. Given that Neddy had no money and received a pittance for sweeping duties, I suggested a punishment that would reflect his realities. Yet viewed from the Bench, he did not look the sort of man one would like to meet in one of the dark lanes that still exist in the old parts of Sydney.

Abe Saffron ran a lot of establishments, reportedly for gambling and consenting adult sexual behaviour. He knew all too well Sydney's weakness for avarice and lust. Once he too appeared before me in the High Court. He looked exactly what he was: a well-dressed, successful businessman. He was a great litigant and deployed the best lawyers of the time, including Sir Garfield Barwick QC. Barwick presented arguments of exquisite subtlety designed to beat 'the system'. Lawyers loved Mr Saffron.

Top-ranking police commissioners make the list in *Sin city*. Corruption of police or anyone else, unless nipped in the bud, poisons a society and is no joking matter. Yet it is never enough to punish those who are caught. A society that is serious about the subject will try to tackle the causes. That means repairing the gulf between the espoused principles of community 'morality' and the activities which the community enjoys pursuing.

I have put 'sin' in quotes because some of the 'sins' recounted in this book are questionable, viewed in retrospect. When I was young, the *Crimes Act 1900* (NSW) contained a number of heavily punished crimes designed to stamp out the 'sin' of homosexuality. Handsome young policemen were deployed to entrap gays in various city parks in the 1950s. The afternoon tabloids, *The Sun* and *The Mirror*, screamed the offences from their front pages. Police Commissioner Delaney, reassuringly incorrupt, pronounced homosexual 'vice' as the greatest evil facing Australia at the time. Yet scattered around Sydney, and doubtless elsewhere, were a small handful of venues where gays could meet with only occasional risks of a police raid. Looking back, some of these may have been owned by Abe Saffron, with his unerring eye for a quick buck.

The SP bookmakers could not be stamped out. So they have now graduated to the TAB. And later came a casino. If we are so inclined, internet gambling on the weirdest odds of events occurring in outer Azerbaijan is available to the modern 'sinner'. Now most do not consider these things 'sins' at all.

The moral of this tale is that the seven deadly sins, and especially lust, gambling and various drugs, are very hard to suppress. Ultimately, we reach a point of asking whether the race is worth the candle. Ponder on this thought as a reality check as you read the stories of the 'sinners' collected in this book.

When I was a judge, I had no problem in punishing severely crimes of violence: homicide, assaults, knives and the rest of it. As for the so-called 'sinning' crimes, at least when committed in private by consenting adults, I dealt with them unenthusiastically. I would do my duty, for it is not the judge's privilege to ignore laws made by parliament. But I would do it with the knowledge, born of my own experience growing up in Sydney, that 'sin' is often in the eye of the beholder. There is an awful lot of it and much hypocrisy about it besides.

Perhaps, in the end, Sydney was not 'Sin City' after all. Just a cosmopolitan, beautiful, generally tolerant and up-to-date place, where people wanted to enjoy life to the full in an environment blessed with the beauties of the world and with people mixed together from its four corners.

INTRODUCTION TIM GIRLING-BUTCHER

Any portrait of a modern capitalist city that focuses on art or architecture and ignores syndicated crime would be like one of those eighteenth century paintings of gentry ladies that embellish the rosy cheeks and ignore the pox scars.

Alfred McCoy, 1986[1]

In the second half of the 20th century, Sin City was a fitting title for Sydney. Organised crime held a grip on the city and corruption was rife, infiltrating the top levels of politics, law and justice.

Central to this corruption were the vice trades – namely gambling, drugs, liquor and prostitution. What began in the early 20th century as a moral crusade against these supposedly sinful trades grew over successive decades into something far more sinister and vulgar than the activities the new laws were trying to stamp out.

The black market was booming and enormous amounts of money could be made. By the mid-seventies the annual turnover of the major vice trades in New South Wales was estimated to be worth more than $2.2 billion (equivalent to $11.2 billion today).[2]

As a result, bribery, blackmail and other more imaginative forms of persuasion were commonplace. Criminals have said on the record that even they couldn't believe how overt corruption became during the peak years. British-born criminal Jim Anderson, who arrived in Sydney in the sixties, described his reaction during an inquiry in the early eighties:

I studied the system pretty closely because I found it, having come from London where things were done a bit more discreetly, that this was a bit blatant. It seemed to be accepted and that was the system.[3]

As corruption became more entrenched it seemed that even public exposure was no deterrent. Headlines such as 'Bribes "protect" gambling clubs'[4] and

PREVIOUS PAGE Topless dancers at Madame's nightclub, Kings Cross, c1966.
© Robert McFarlane

'Mafia link with NSW crime'[5] began appearing in Sydney's newspapers in the early seventies, but initially were met with little government reaction. Police and politicians continued to deny the existence of organised crime.

But a change in government in the mid-seventies, combined with a number of high-profile scandals, forced change. Legislation was loosened, illegal casinos were closed and slowly the traditional sources of bribe money were reduced.

While by no means a comprehensive history, or a complete list of the key players, the following pages provide an insight into some of the personalities and activities that gave Sydney its reputation as one of the most corrupt cities in the Western world.

THE ORIGINS OF ORGANISED CRIME IN SYDNEY

Razorhurst, Gunhurst, Bottlehurst, Dopehurst – it used to be Darlinghurst, one of the finest quarters of a rich and beautiful city; today it is a plague spot where the spawn of the gutter grow and fatten on official apathy.

The Truth, 1928[6]

The development of organised crime in Sydney depended on two important factors: prohibition and population. The temperance movement swept through Australia at the beginning of the 20th century, resulting in new laws banning many of the activities and commodities that Sydneysiders had long enjoyed.

Prohibition forced hotels to close at 6pm and on Sundays, it became illegal for prostitutes to solicit on the street, and practically all forms of gambling were outlawed. To place a bet, legislation required a person to be physically present at one of the few licensed racecourses in the state.

Drugs such as heroin and cocaine were also banned. Previously these had been openly available from chemists at bargain prices. A 1919 report stated that 4.5 grams of cocaine, which today would have a street value of several thousand dollars, could be purchased for 5 shillings – just $16 today.[7]

11

The second factor was size. Syndicated crime requires a large population to serve as its consumer base and to allow its members to move about unnoticed. Between 1901 and 1926 Sydney doubled in size to more than 1 million people.[8] Additionally an expanded public transport system gave residents increased mobility. Many inner-city dwellers moved from congested terrace housing to the suburbs. Between 1921 and 1929 the number of City of Sydney residents actually fell from 103,160 to 90,879.[9]

The effect on inner-city neighbourhoods was dramatic. As the city focused on its new suburbs, the areas around East Sydney and Darlinghurst were transformed into slums, becoming the centre for the vice trades. By the late 1920s sly-grog dealing (illegal alcohol sales), prostitution, SP bookmaking ('starting price', or off-track betting) and cocaine dealing thrived.

Three syndicates dominated the city during this period. One was headed by Phil 'the Jew' Jeffs, and the others by two powerful women able to work a loophole in the law. It was illegal for a man but not a woman to profit from the work of prostitutes, and Kate Leigh and Tilly Devine rose to dominance.

With a booming vice economy Sydney's syndicate leaders could now earn more money managing crimes than committing them. Vicious battles took place as they fought one another for greater territory. A signature of these battles were L-shaped scars on victims' faces, as gun laws had made cut-throat razors the weapon of choice.

Unlike the syndicates that started dominating the city in the sixties, these early groups commanded only limited political influence to protect their operations. The sight of both razor scars and an ever-increasing number of cocaine junkies wandering the city's streets created community outrage and the government was forced to act. The *New South Wales Vagrancy Act* was amended in 1929 with the introduction of the 'consorting' clause, by which it became illegal to 'habitually consort with reputed thieves, or prostitutes, or persons who have no visible or lawful means of support'.[10]

Over the following ten years police aggressively pursued syndicate members, making repeated arrests, many of which were followed by harsh sentences. By the outbreak of World War II police had successfully broken up the main syndicates and almost entirely wiped out the narcotics trade. Gambling, drinking and sex, however, were to remain as popular as ever.

WORLD WAR II AND THE AMERICAN INFLUENCE

> *The US Army authorities could and should help the courts by restricting the amount of money their men carry. By their excessive spending power they upset the even distribution of controlled goods, such as tobacco and liquor, undermine the steadfastness of our young women, encourage unseemly disturbances in our public thoroughfares and lead to these serious crimes.*
>
> Judge's summary in a 1944 assault case against three men accused of beating a US soldier[11]

From 1942 Sydney became the temporary home to thousands of cashed-up American servicemen either stationed in the city or passing through on leave. Their base monthly wage of £18 (equal to about $1100 today) was twice that of their Aussie counterparts.[12] By the time they arrived in Sydney they could have several months back pay with only a week or two to spend it.

Among their priorities were gambling, drinking and sex, all of which could be obtained on the black market. Compounding the existing restrictions was wartime rationing. Beer supply dropped by 40 per cent due to reduced production and the need to supply troops offshore, the importation of spirits was banned and pubs were supplied with a set quota of liquor that often ran dry.

Although prices were regulated by the government, the cost of drinking soared as demand outstripped supply and people looked for a quick dollar. A publican could make an extra £2 ($100) per dozen bottles of beer above the government-set price if he sold it out the back door. Sly-grog dealers were reported to be selling beer at up to £6 ($350) per dozen, local spirits at £4 ($234) per bottle and scotch at £7 ($410) a bottle.[13]

Businesses such as the Roosevelt Club in Kings Cross and Romano's restaurant in Martin Place thrived during this period as they found ways to exploit opportunities presented by the war. By providing a late-night venue under the guise of a restaurant, clubs attracted patrons with money in their pockets and hearts set on having a good time. Booze and cash flowed.

Abe Saffron began his career when he took over the Roosevelt in 1943, and despite its being shut down by court order in 1944, he re-opened and operated the venue until the early fifties.

Much of this activity was examined by the Maxwell Royal Commission into liquor laws in New South Wales, which ran from 1951–54. At the beginning of the commission Saffron owned a network of hotels, with family members or friends acting as fronts. He used these hotels to supply his Roosevelt Restaurant and Nightclub with liquor, beer mostly – at least 3000 bottles a week.[14]

ABOVE **Romano's restaurant. Photographer unknown, 1946.** Mitchell Library, State Library of New South Wales

Despite lying to the commission and having his illegal operations exposed, Saffron managed to avoid prosecution. The Roosevelt, however, was declared a disorderly house and closed down before the commission ended.[15]

The commission also looked at police. Maxwell discovered that a 'laissez-faire' attitude had developed among many New South Wales police officers toward sly-grog dealing, and that highly suspicious relationships had formed between a few key police officers and those dealing in liquor. Two senior officers in particular were identified as having been given lavish retirement parties and presented with large cheques — £600 ($25,000) and £1000 ($42,000) respectively – drawn by bookmakers and pub and club owners.[16] Others were found to have more wealth than could be attributed to their salaries, and no plausible explanations for it.

BOOKIES AND BACCARAT

> *To reach the back yard man you walked down a lane and turned along another and then into the yard of a terrace house. A newspaper form guide was tacked to the fence and the prices were displayed on a sheet of paper clipped to the clothesline . . . Through a window in the laundry these clean cut young men, staff men for the big fellow, recorded your bets with your initials or your first name.*

Sydney Morning Herald on the end of the SP bookie after the opening of the TAB, 1968[17]

Illegal gambling remained one of the biggest earners for the underworld. Gambling houses where the card game baccarat and the coin game two-up were played[18] had flourished across the city since World War II and people spent big money in them. Evidence given during a 1965 court case revealed that a Sydney solicitor lost £50,000 ($1.09 million) between 1962 and 1964 in four city baccarat schools.[19]

Illegal bookmaking was also a major source of income. Thousands of keen punters across the state lived far from racetracks, leaving them with no legal way to place a bet. Instead they turned to the local illegal SP bookmakers operating out of pubs and backyards and over the phone.

In the big western city he was Ray, the stout, florid-faced man in the grey cardigan who took your bets over the phone a couple of minutes before they jumped. He was fast and efficient and made no comment but the droll repetition of 'five by five so and so' or 'ten straight this or that'. [20]

The 1963 report of the royal commission into off-course betting estimated that £275 million ($6.4 billion) was being put through illegal bookmakers each year.

A key recommendation of the royal commission was the establishment of the TAB (Totalisator Agency Board) to combat illegal SP bookies and direct some of that money to the government. Opening on 9 December 1964, the TAB turned over £4.8 million ($107.4 million) in its first six months – nearly double what the Victorian TAB had taken in its first six months of business, and above the £1 million taken during the same period in Queensland, but well short of the royal commission's estimates.[21] Millions of pounds would continue to pass through illegal bookies for some time to come.[22]

CORRUPTION AND BAD MANAGEMENT

During the eleven years from 1965 to 1976, with the Liberal-Country Parties in power, the state endured a period of political and police corruption unparalleled in its modern history.

Alfred McCoy, 1980[23]

The change of government in New South Wales in 1965 was a key moment in the evolution of organised crime. Sir Robert Askin was voted in as Premier with his Liberal-Country coalition, and over the following decade the black-market economy and corruption in New South Wales became entrenched.

At the same time a number of murders took place as Sydney criminals battled for control of the lucrative vice market. Most prominent were the violent killings of Richard Reilly, who owned several baccarat schools in Kings Cross, and prostitute overlord Joe Borg.

Reilly was shot as he left his mistress's flat in Double Bay on the evening of 26 June 1967 and his death was a turning point in the development of organised crime. With Reilly gone, many of the city's baccarat schools transformed from easy-to-disguise gambling houses into substantial 'Las Vegas'-style plush casinos.

Joe Borg was killed in one of Australia's first car-bomb murders on 28 May 1968 as he started his car outside his Bondi home. Borg owned a number of houses in the red-light strip of Palmer Street, Darlinghurst. Police claimed he was renting rooms to prostitutes for $20 ($200) per eight-hour shift and that he was clearing $8000–$10,000 ($80,000–$100,000) per week. After his death his houses immediately shut for business while his estate was put in order (he left everything to the RSPCA) and prostitutes were reported to be paying $48 per shift due to the sudden lack of accommodation.[24] Before long, massage parlours and 'health clinics' sprang up all over Sydney as fronts for prostitution.

Illegal casinos were pivotal in corrupting police and politicians. In 1974 a Sydney University economics lecturer, Dr Geoffrey Lewis, compiled statistics on one of Perc Galea's casinos in Double Bay. By visiting the establishment three nights a week for just short of a year, he estimated that the casino's five roulette wheels, six blackjack tables and one craps table were turning over $2 million ($13 million) a week. He totalled the tax-free profit derived from that turnover to be close to $15 million ($99 million) a year after expenses.

With such substantial set-ups there was no easy way these casinos could have disguised their operations should the police have decided to raid. In order to operate, they needed friends in high places. Staff revealed to Dr Lewis that on top of weekly outgoings of $10,000 ($66,300) in wages and $1000 ($6600) in rent, $5000 ($33,000) was being spent bribing senior police and politicians.[25]

David Hickie claimed Premier Askin and his police commissioners were each taking $100,000 (more than $1 million) a year in bribes to leave the casinos alone.[26] Casinos continued to operate freely despite the repeated publication of their locations by the press, and continual questioning in parliament as to

why the government wasn't closing them down. It could be argued that the authorities, if not actually corrupt, were failing dismally at their jobs. 'Ministers are busy people who cannot be expected to disrupt their tight schedules merely to read Sydney newspapers wherein, regularly, they would discover the addresses of the city's casinos', a 1974 editorial lamented.[27]

Much of this activity was overseen by the underworld characters who had benefited from the deaths of Borg and Reilly, including Lennie McPherson, George Freeman, Stan Smith and Frederick 'Paddles' Anderson. They controlled or had a stake in pretty much anything illegal that earned a dollar and took place in Sydney, although they claimed to draw the line at drugs.

ABOVE Staff from Hobart's Wrest Point casino give a promotional demonstration in Sydney in the 1970s. © Fairfax Photos

RE-EMERGENCE OF THE DRUG TRADE

*Eight hits today man. Haven't eaten for six days. It's fuckin'
incredible in the Cross today – the shit scene. A couple of months
ago a cap of H was $20. Now it's $35. As the squad busts pushers,
it sends the price right up.*

Kings Cross junkie, 1971[28]

Sydney's relationship with drugs started changing as a second surge of
American servicemen, this time on R and R from Vietnam, came to the city.

Between 1967 and 1971, more than 280,000 servicemen visited Sydney,
with up to 7500 of them in the city at any one time. They injected $80 million
(equivalent to $707 million today) into the local economy, much of it around
Kings Cross.[29]

This influx of servicemen shared the previous generation's desires for late-
night venues, booze, women and betting, but also brought a new and recently
acquired appetite – for heroin and marijuana.[30] 'Some 20 percent of our military
personnel may be marijuana users and upwards to 10 percent of our personnel
in Vietnam could be using hard narcotics,'[31] a US House of Representatives
report said in 1971.

Sydney hadn't had a drug problem since the 1930s, but once re-established,
the local markets flourished by exploiting the same corrupt networks and
contacts that had already been established by the casinos and SP betting
rings. Drug dealing would eventually emerge as one of the major income
streams for the underworld.

By 1976–77, the turnover generated by the major vice trades was huge:
narcotics at $59 million ($266 million), SP bookmaking at $1.42 billion
($6.4 billion), illegal casinos at $650 million ($2.9 billion) and poker-machine
'skimming' at $90 million ($406 million). Of this, an estimated $1.4 million
($6.3 million) was being spent on bribing police and politicians.[32]

Between 1976 and 1978 the number of heroin users in New South Wales grew by 24 per cent and by the mid-eighties the drug trade was worth $2 billion ($4.679 billion) a year.[33] The likes of Murray Riley (an ex-cop), David Kelleher, the Mr Asia syndicate, Bruce 'Snapper' Cornwell, Robert Trimbole and Neddy Smith imported and distributed vast quantities of heroin and cannabis.[34]

EXPOSURE BY THE MEDIA

> *Instead of controversy about politics and administration, you find questions being asked if someone has shares in some company and if he once had lunch with Mr Barton [a corrupt businessman] or some such thing. I don't think that matters a damn and I don't think the man in the street wants to know about it as much as he wants to know about what the government is doing for him.*

Sir Robert Askin at the time of his retirement, 1975[35]

Public exposure could be the greatest threat to corruption, and if not for the fearless work of a few public servants, journalists and newspapers, Sydney could have become a far more sinister place than it is today.

An early example of this was a story by journalists Bob Bottom and Tony Reeves, titled 'The night the Mafia came to Australia', published in the *Daily Telegraph* in 1972. The article detailed allegations about the American Mafia and the Sydney underworld infiltrating Sydney clubs. Poker machines had been legal in New South Wales clubs since 1956 and the state had almost as many machines as Nevada, home state of Las Vegas.[36] Once inside such clubs, criminals such as Murray Riley (p106) were able to influence crucial decisions regarding key appointments, the purchasing of poker machines and the contracting out of services.

A media frenzy ensued, forcing the Askin government to establish the Moffitt Royal Commission into organised crime in clubs. The final report, published in 1974, found that organised criminals had in fact infiltrated clubs and were extorting money, but Moffitt also looked at the lessons learned in the United

States and Britain when dealing with organised crime. He was one of the first officials to warn the government about the rise of organised crime:

> *A weapon of organised crime is by planning to avoid generating evidence of its crimes, or if there is evidence, to suppress it by intimidation or corruption. However there is at times other evidence of varying quality that crimes, not provable in court, are or may be occurring, or that criminals are operating within legitimate business.*[37]

Moffitt's words were ignored. A few years earlier, Commissioner Norman Allan had set in motion an operation by the New South Wales police to illegally tap phones. In 1984, Melbourne's *The Age* newspaper published selected transcripts taken from phone-tap material recorded between 1976 and 1983. Bob Bottom, who passed the transcripts to *The Age*, described their contents in an interview that year.

> *After all, the people who are taped are organised crime czars ... They are the people who do kill people and in fact there are direct references out of their own mouths talking about bumping people off – they run the heroin trade of Australia, they run the brothels, they fix the races, they burn down premises for arson and all of it so far is ignored, yet you have it from them in their own words.*[38]

The story was huge, with more than 800 names implicated in the material and some people comparing it to America's Watergate scandal. Many, including the police, denied the tapes were real but they were eventually authenticated by Justice Donald Stewart. Strangely, the government was more concerned about the legality of the tapes rather than the crimes they exposed and calls for a royal commission were ignored.

A CHANGE OF CULTURE

> *... the ultimate say in combating organised crime rests with the parliament, not the police.*
>
> Journalist Bob Bottom, 1979[39]

Throughout the seventies and into the early eighties both police and politicians had been continually denying the existence of organised crime. But following scandals such as the Bill Allen affair (p58) and *The Age* tapes, this stance became difficult to maintain.

Additionally, the exposure of serious misconduct committed by Detective Sergeant Roger Rogerson and his colleagues such as Detective Sergeant Bill Duff saw a major change in the police force. John Avery, who was appointed Police Commissioner in 1984, started by breaking up the worst areas of corruption, such as the Central Investigation Bureau, and investigating allegations against individual police: 'There was a culture shock about people getting locked up … Most of our corrupt cases were associated with police being involved with drug trafficking.'[40]

Following on from the Moffitt Royal Commission came the Woodward, Williams, Costigan and Stewart royal commissions, whose strong recommendations on the means of combating organised crime were finally acted on by the federal government in 1984. Where other countries had federal crime-fighting bodies that were charged with independently investigating corruption across state borders—such as the FBI in the United States—Australia only had the Federal Police, whose powers were limited by comparison.

Under the leadership of Justice Don Stewart, the National Crime Authority (NCA; now a part of the Australian Crime Commission) was established to fill this gap and was given broad powers to actively investigate and prosecute criminals country-wide. While the role the NCA played in combating organised crime has been fiercely debated, it jailed Lennie McPherson for conspiracy to have an associate beaten, and was the only organisation ever to put Abe Saffron behind bars.

Similarly, in New South Wales the NSW Crime Commission was formed, which had the power to confiscate assets if the Supreme Court ruled it probable they had been earned through crime. Additionally the Independent Commission Against Corruption (ICAC) was created in 1988. In the 1990s it exposed many of the corrupt relationships between New South Wales police and criminals and was followed shortly after by the Wood Royal Commission, initiating major operational changes to the New South Wales police force.

How successful these changes were in completely ridding the city of its corrupt culture is still hotly debated to this day, mainly because many of the allegations were never fully investigated at the time. Some see an absence of convictions as proof of innocence, while others regard this as merely a dynamic of organised crime. As Justice Moffitt said in 1974:

> *There may be sufficient material to be satisfied that there has been some assault, or threat or bribe, yet the participants or victims when interviewed will not provide admissible evidence of the crime.*

Perhaps the only definitive conclusion that can be drawn is that laws restricting access to popular activities and commodities failed to seriously affect the public's appetite for them. In the end it was our desire to have a drink, or to place a bet on a horse, a coin, the roulette wheel or the pokies, that bankrolled organised crime.

NOTES

1 Alfred McCoy in Jim Davidson (ed), *The Sydney–Melbourne book*, Allen & Unwin, Sydney, 1986, p97.

2 Alfred McCoy, *Drug traffic: narcotics and organized crime in Australia*, Harper & Row, Sydney, 1980, p200.

3 Tony Reeves, *Mr Sin*, Allen & Unwin, Sydney, 2007, p71.

4 *Sydney Morning Herald*, 21 June 1973.

5 *Sydney Morning Herald*, 21 August 1973.

6 Quoted by Alfred McCoy in Jim Davidson (ed), *The Sydney–Melbourne book*, Allen & Unwin, Sydney, 1986, p104.

7 Alfred McCoy, *Drug traffic: narcotics and organized crime in Australia*, Harper & Row, Sydney, 1980, p41.

8 Australian Bureau of Statistics, 3105.0.65.001 Australian Historical Population Statistics, 2008.

9 Peter Spearritt, *Sydney since the twenties*, Hale & Iremonger, Sydney, 1978, p33.

10 Alfred McCoy, *Drug traffic: narcotics and organized crime in Australia*, Harper & Row, Sydney, 1980, p137.

11 *The Sun*, 13 March 1944.

12 Barry Ralph, *They passed this way*, Kangaroo Press, Sydney, 2000, p46.

13 *The Sun*, 8 December 1944.

14 *Report*, Royal Commission on liquor laws, New South Wales Parliament, p71.

15 *The Sun*, 21 January 1953.

16 *Report*, Royal Commission on liquor laws, New South Wales Parliament, p98.

17 Joe Glascott, *Sydney Morning Herald*, 28 September 1968.

18 *Sun-Herald*, 13 June 1982.

19 Alfred McCoy, *Drug traffic: narcotics and organized crime in Australia*, Harper & Row, Sydney, 1980, p185.

20 *Sydney Morning Herald*, 28 September 1968.

21 *Sydney Morning Herald*, 8 June 1965.

22 *Sydney Morning Herald*, 11 May 1968.

23 Alfred McCoy, *Drug traffic: narcotics and organized crime in Australia*, Harper & Row, Sydney, 1980, p199.

24 *Sydney Morning Herald*, 31 May 1968 and 8 December 1970.

25 Alfred McCoy, *Drug traffic: narcotics and organized crime in Australia*, Harper & Row, Sydney, 1980, p199.

26 David Hickie, *The prince and the premier*, Angus & Robertson, Sydney, 1985, p59.

27 *Sydney Morning Herald*, 30 July 1974.

28 Rennie Ellis and Wesley Stacey, *Kings Cross Sydney*, Thomas Nelson (Australia) Ltd, Melbourne, 1971, p61.

29 *Sydney Morning Herald*, 7 December 1971.

30 *Sun-Herald*, 10 November 1968; *Sydney Morning Herald*, 11 June 1971.

31 *Sydney Morning Herald*, 29 August 1971.

32 Alfred McCoy, *Drug traffic: narcotics and organized crime in Australia*, Harper & Row, Sydney, 1980, p200.

33 Evan Whitton, *Can of worms II*, Fairfax Library, 1987, p125; *Sydney Morning Herald*, 25 August 1985.

34 Clive Small and Tom Gilling, *Smack express*, Allen & Unwin, Sydney, pp43–53.

35 David Hickie, *The prince and the premier*, Angus & Robertson, Sydney, 1985, p75.

36 Bob Bottom, *The Godfather in Australia*, Reed, 1979, p40; *Without fear or favour*, Sun Books, Melbourne, 1984, p31.

37 *Report*, Allegations of Organised Crime in Clubs, New South Wales Government Printer, 1974, p43.

38 *Sydney Morning Herald*, 31 August 1984.

39 Bob Bottom, *The Godfather in Australia*, Reed, 1979, p111.

40 *Sydney Morning Herald*, 10 June 1989.

OVERLEAF Sir Wayne Martin at the Pink Pussycat Club, Kings Cross, 1970–71. © Rennie Ellis Photographic Archive

THE PLAYGROUND

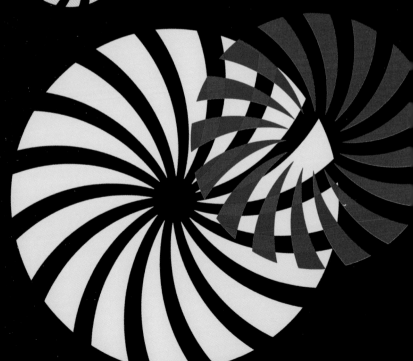

LEFT The dance floor of the Roosevelt Club – one of the venues in which US servicemen were said to regularly undermine 'the steadfastness of our young women' – in 1944. Image courtesy Alan Saffron

ABOVE The Roosevelt Club in Orwell Street, Kings Cross, 1940s. The building still stands, and is now a restaurant. Image courtesy National Library of Australia

Described by Justice Maxwell as one of Sydney's 'most infamous nighclubs', the Roosevelt flouted the state's strict liquor laws. Opening in 1940, the club sold liquor illegally and at 'extortionate prices', making the most of the economic boom that followed the arrival in Sydney of thousands of cashed-up American servicemen. Abe Saffron (p110) took it over in the mid-forties and its operations became a key focus of the 1952–54 royal commission into liquor. It remained a favourite haunt for Sydney's social elite until it was forcibly closed in 1953.

ABOVE Kate Leigh and Tilly Devine, 20 August 1948. © Fairfax Photos

RIGHT Confiscated liquor, Sydney, 14 June 1952. © Fairfax Photos

On top of cocaine and prostitution, Kate Leigh and Tilly Devine (p12) made considerable profit from the sale of illicit alcohol, known as 'sly grog'. The six o'clock pub closures and the illegality of Sunday trading guaranteed thousands of customers as Sydneysiders turned to the black market for their liquor.

While liquor supplies were rationed and prices set by the government, publicans would often sell liquor out of the back door at heavily marked-up prices to dealers and clubs. They in turn would on-sell it at a higher price. Newspaper reports from the 1940s claimed that people were paying as much as £6 (equivalent to $350 today) for a dozen bottles of beer.

ABOVE **Private meeting, Kings Cross, 1970–71.** © Rennie Ellis Photographic Archive

RIGHT **The top of William Street, 1970.** Photographer unknown. National Archives of Australia A1200, L84008

LEFT Working girl, Kings Cross, 1970–71. © Rennie Ellis Photographic Archive

ABOVE Police photograph of a room used to carry out abortions, 9 December 1959.
New South Wales Police Forensic Photography Archive, Justice and Police Museum,
Historic Houses Trust of New South Wales

Women were often heavily exploited by the activities of organised crime in Sydney as lucrative rackets grew around prostitution and abortions. Prostitutes were often forced to pay money both to a standover man to ensure their physical safety and to corrupt police to ensure they were not arrested. If they couldn't pay, they ended up either beaten or in prison. Dependencies on drugs were also exploited to keep women working in the trade.

Abortion rackets greatly benefited the men who operated them, while placing the lives of their female patients at considerable risk. The wealthy playboy Dr Reginald Stuart-Jones (1902–1961) is alleged to have made a fortune from an illegal abortion racket, working in collaboration with corrupt members of the New South Wales police force.

Property of Hells Angels, Kings Cross, 1970–71. © Rennie Ellis Photographic Archive

The Pink Panther, Kings Cross, 1970–71. © Rennie Ellis Photographic Archive

38

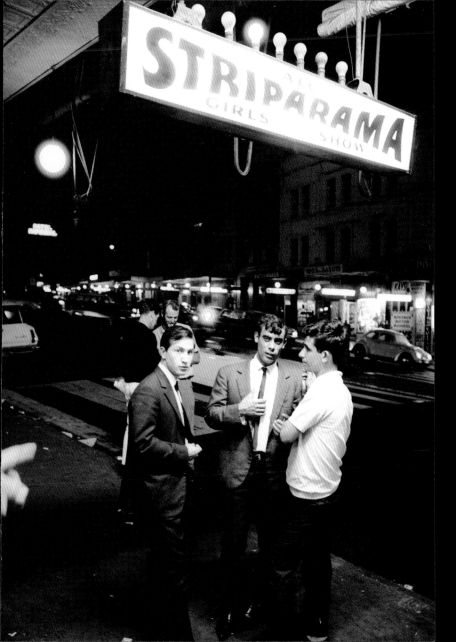

40   **Go-go dancer, Kings Cross, 1970–71.** © Wesley Stacey

ABOVE Carlotta, one of the most celebrated female impersonators at the Kings Cross club Les Girls, c1970. © Wesley Stacey

OVERLEAF Performers get ready in a Kings Cross club, 1970–71. © Rennie Ellis Photographic Archive

ABOVE American servicemen on R and R, Kings Cross, c1970. © Fairfax Photos

RIGHT American serviceman and friend, Kings Cross, 1970–71. © Rennie Ellis Photographic Archive

Between 1967 and 1971, 280,000 American servicemen visited Sydney on rest and recreation leave from Vietnam, spending an estimated $80 million (equivalent to $707 million today) – most of it in Kings Cross. Drugs hadn't been a serious problem in Sydney since the thirties, but this also changed with the arrival of the servicemen. Karl Bonnette (p69), who was working in clubs in the Cross during this period, said in a 2009 interview with the Historic Houses Trust that this was when drug use started to take off: 'The only real problem was what they brought into the Cross, the drugs … Heroin was the one that they brought in. And heavier pills, quaaludes and stuff like that, we'd never heard of them.'

LEFT Red Baron regulars, Kings Cross, 1970–71. © Rennie Ellis Photographic Archive
ABOVE Spruiker, Kings Cross, 13 April 1978. © Fairfax Photos

LEFT A punter lays odds with bookmaker Terry Page at Randwick racecourse, Sydney, 9 September 1972. © Fairfax Photos

ABOVE Racegoers watch the Melbourne Cup on television at Randwick racecourse, Sydney, 3 November 1970. © Fairfax Photos

If not handled correctly, a big punter could break a bookie. In his book *The prince and the premier,* David Hickie outlined the spectacular duels that took place between Perc Galea (p86) and Terry Page (left). Between 1975 and 1977 Galea took more than $395,000 (equivalent to $1.78 million today) from Page in winnings. Page survived his losses while Galea's life was ended by a heart attack in 1977.

A 'cockatoo' guards the door of an illegal gambling house at 28 Kellett Street, Kings Cross, 23 December 1987. © Fairfax Photos

A hidden miniature camera was used to take this picture at an illegal casino in Bondi Junction, Sydney, in December 1977. © Fairfax Photos

51

LEFT Jack Rooklyn, c1975. © Fairfax Photos

ABOVE People play the poker machines at South Sydney Junior Rugby League Club, 2 August 1983. © Fairfax Photos

Poker machines were legalised in New South Wales clubs in 1956 and very quickly attracted the attention of criminal groups. Bally Australia, headed by Jack Rooklyn, became a major player in the supply of gaming machines, resulting in its activities being examined by the Moffitt Royal Commission of 1973–74. Moffitt found that Bally had strong connections with international criminals and said that if Bally was not stopped, organised crime would soon dominate the industry.

Moffitt also found that local criminals had infiltrated clubs such as South Sydney Junior Rugby League Club (pictured above) and were exploiting the clubs' massive incomes in a way that typified 'the US gangster pattern', by skimming profits and subcontracting out business to their own companies.

ABOVE **(from left) George Freeman (p85), Dr Nick Paltos (later jailed for importing drugs) and the then Chief Stipendiary Magistrate Murray Farquhar (p81) in the members stand at Randwick racecourse in 1977.** Anonymous source

Following the publication of this photo, it was revealed that Farquhar was receiving regular racing tips from Freeman, who was allegedly fixing the races. According to Farquhar's clerk, who put the money on for Farquhar and got the winnings back, Freeman's tips were 98–99 per cent accurate.

George Freeman was alleged to have been one of the biggest SP bookmakers, operating with police protection. In the year 1976–77, illegal SP bookmakers were estimated to be turning over $1.4 billion (equivalent to $6.4 billion today) despite the existence of the TAB. After a period of inaction, a team of New South Wales police headed by Merv Beck brought about a leap in the number of arrests. In September 1981, 21 Division, which was responsible for policing illegal gambling, made only five arrests, whereas over the following four months 'Beck's Raiders' made more than 1000.

THE PLAYERS

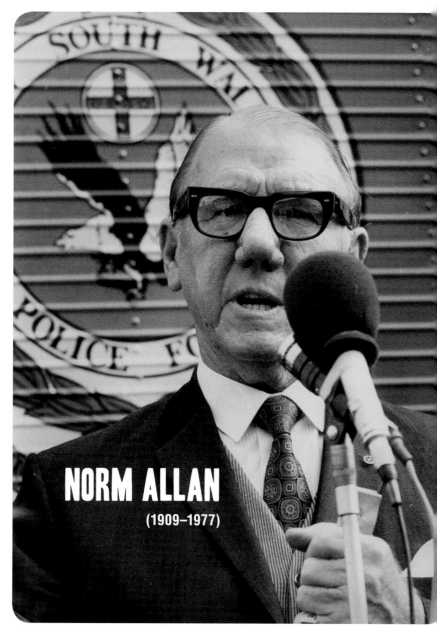

NORM ALLAN

(1909–1977)

NEW SOUTH WALES POLICE COMMISSIONER 1962–1972

At the age of 52 Norman Allan became the youngest man to lead the force when in 1962 he was appointed police commissioner.

Illegal casinos boomed while he was in charge, leading many to claim he was corrupt. A close associate of Perc Galea (p86) told journalist David Hickie that Allan was paid $100,000 (equivalent to $1 million today) a year in bribes to leave the casinos open.[1] Allan also supplied a report to the government saying there was no illegal gambling in Broken Hill, 'despite the clearest evidence and common knowledge that the contrary was the case'.[2]

His leadership was at times unorthodox. In 1969 he was awarded the Queen's Commendation for Brave Conduct for his bizarre handling of the 1966 Glenfield siege. Having taken his girlfriend and their child hostage, a 22-year-old gunman began making odd demands to police. Allan took control personally, and to the Police Association's horror supplied the man with an Armalite (M16) rifle with 200 bullets. He also arranged for the man and his hostage to be married, overseeing the ceremony and acting as witness. The siege finally ended after seven days with no casualties.

Allan was forced to retire from the force in 1972 after the Askin government withdrew support for him following the Arantz scandal (p65).[3]

Norm Allan delivering a speech in Sydney, 12 May 1972. © Fairfax Photos

NEW SOUTH WALES POLICE FORCE c1942–1982

In just a few years Bill Allen leap-frogged many of his more senior colleagues, rising from a sergeant in the Criminal Investigation Bureau to deputy commissioner, the second most powerful cop in the force. To this day he remains the most senior New South Wales police officer to have been jailed for corruption.

A 1982 police tribunal found 'Allen did act in a manner likely to bring discredit upon the police force'.[2] He received multiple visits from 'major crime figure'[3] Abe Saffron (p110) at police headquarters, and paid $2500 to a licensing officer who policed the Darlinghurst/Kings Cross area: '... the sergeant claims that Mr Allen shook hands with him and, in doing so, pressed an envelope containing money into his hand.'[4]

Allen's family flew first class to the United States at no charge on tickets arranged by the Queanbeyan Leagues Club, which was lobbying for support in opening up a casino. While in Las Vegas they stayed at Caesar's Palace, where Allen met with Jack Rooklyn (p53), who also paid their bill.

Despite the seriousness of the inquiry's findings, Allen was not dismissed from the force. Instead he negotiated a comfortable retirement package comprising $37,000 in cash (equivalent to $105,000 today) and an annual pension of $17,000 ($48,500).[5]

In 1992, at the age of 70, he was jailed for 18 months for his attempt to bribe the licensing officer. Abe Saffron was charged with being responsible for the payments but avoided prosecution.

Bill Allen in Sydney, 7 May 1979. © Fairfax Photos

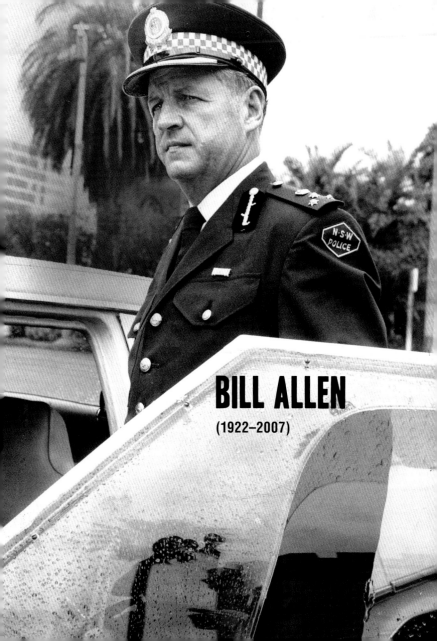

BILL ALLEN

(1922–2007)

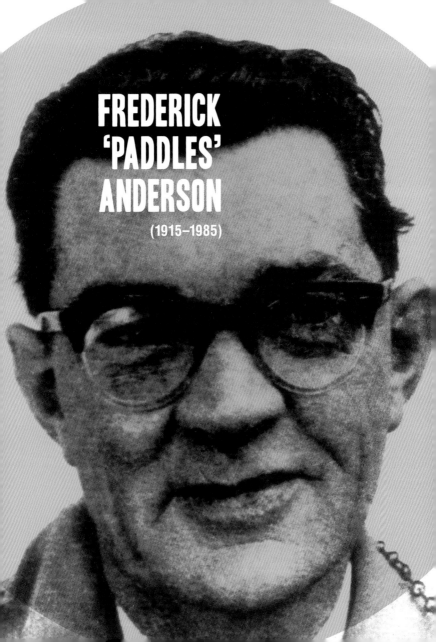

FREDERICK
'PADDLES'
ANDERSON
(1915–1985)

> **Paddles was a true Australian godfather, the rarely acknowledged titular head of the entrenched underworld of Sydney, with control also over events in Queensland, if not Victoria.**
>
> Bob Bottom, 1985[1]

Very little was known about 'Paddles' Anderson's role in Sydney crime until material from *The Age* tapes was made public in 1985.

The tapes, which New South Wales police recorded illegally between 1976 and 1983, identified who was who in Sydney's underworld and the nature of their operations. They clearly showed for the first time Anderson's senior position within the Sydney underworld.

One conversation illustrated how Anderson organised for money to go to Lennie McPherson (p98) in return for protecting a new illegal casino from police and standover men. When told the caller's contact wished to expand his Sydney operations, Anderson offered a warning: 'Well let me tell you something. If he's got that in mind he's gonna have a very short life span. It won't last. You don't take over other people's things …'.[2]

He was alleged to have been a close associate of Detective Inspector Ray Kelly (p94) and to have had powerful contacts within the Labor Party, including former premier and governor general William McKell. Gunman Chow Hayes claimed Anderson once took a group of criminals to a party at the premier's house: 'by the time we arrived half a dozen other thieves were already there. And that was where I first met the infamous medical criminal, Dr Reginald Stuart-Jones.'[3] Stuart-Jones was alleged to have run some of the city's most lucrative abortion rackets along with Ray Kelly.

'[Anderson] was a great guy, he really was,' Karl Bonnette (p69) stated in a 2009 interview. 'And he had plenty of influence in this town. Both with the police, the politicians, the underworld, the over world, everybody, he had connections everywhere.'[4]

Mug shot of Frederick Anderson, date unknown. Anonymous source

> *He's a dog, he's a fucking dog ... the guy robbed Abe*
> *and lived the high life – Rolls Royce, this and that, and*
> *then he gave him up – that's a dog.*

Sir Wayne Martin[1]

Glasgow-born Anderson compiled an interesting résumé before becoming a criminal heavyweight in Sydney's Kings Cross. He claimed he had worked as a traffic policeman in New Zealand, that he had served as a British commando and that as a young man he had graduated as a qualified hair stylist.[2]

He moved to Kings Cross in the late sixties and began working closely with Abe Saffron (p110), running many of his business interests and looking after the books. The pair fell out in the early eighties, leading Anderson to use his inside knowledge against Saffron. It was Anderson's testimony that led to the National Crime Authority's successful prosecution of Saffron for tax evasion.

Anderson was a key witness in the Juanita Nielsen (p101) inquest, with many claiming he was involved in her disappearance. He was the manager of the Carousel Club where Nielsen was allegedly last seen alive, and he was connected to all the other suspects who would have benefited from her death. He also used the inquest to transform his own role from suspect to informer. It was while appearing as a witness at the inquest that he first disclosed the existence of two sets of accounting records – white (doctored) for the tax office, and black (showing actual amounts received and paid, including bribes) – at many of Saffron's establishments.

In 1970 he killed standover man Donny 'The Glove' Smith. Although he admitted to this and even took part in a re-enactment of the crime for television, a charge of manslaughter was dropped. He also claimed to have chased Mr Asia boss Terrence Clark (p73) out of Kings Cross with a shotgun after hearing he was drinking in one of his bars.

Jim Anderson in Kings Cross, Sydney, 26 April 1986. © Fairfax Photos

JIM
ANDERSON
(1930–2003)

PHILIP ARANTZ

(1929–1998)

> *I did what any reasonable police officer would have done under the circumstances … I hope that what I've done, although I will probably be a casualty, will lead to a better police force.*

Detective Sergeant Philip Arantz, 1972[1]

NEW SOUTH WALES POLICE FORCE 1945–1972

Detective Sergeant Philip Arantz was one of Australia's pioneering whistleblowers on police corruption. On 26 November 1971 the *Sydney Morning Herald* published crime statistics leaked by Arantz which showed that Police Commissioner Norman Allan (p57) had been lying about the real crime clear-up rate. The move cost Arantz dearly.

On the day the story broke Commissioner Allan had Arantz forcibly admitted to a psychiatric ward for three days observation in an attempt to discredit him (the police doctor responsible for declaring him 'mentally ill' later confessed that senior police acting on Allan's instructions had coerced him into doing so[2]). Premier Robert Askin (p66) attacked Arantz publicly, saying that if he wasn't ill and had released the figures deliberately 'he deserves nothing but contempt'[3]. He was offered a full pension if he resigned quietly as 'medically unfit'. Arantz declined and was sacked from the force.[4]

Despite Commissioner Allan confirming just ten months later that the leaked figures were in fact correct, it took nearly 20 years for Arantz to clear his name. In 1985 the Wran government paid him $250,000 in compensation (well short of the $1 million it was estimated he should have received) but upheld the decision to sack him. In 1989 the Greiner government notionally reinstated him into the police force, with all references to misconduct, suspension and dismissal expunged.[5]

Philip Arantz at his home in Ryde, Sydney, 13 May 1982. © Fairfax Photos

> *I don't believe in royal commissions. I believe that the people who are seeking royal commissions are out to destroy the reputation of the police force as a prelude to breaking down our system of law and order.*

Sir Robert Askin[1]

NEW SOUTH WALES PREMIER 1965–1975

The day before Sir Robert William Askin's body was cremated, the *National Times* published an article under the headline 'Askin: Friend to organised crime'.

During the ten years that Askin was premier, corruption in New South Wales became institutionalised. Illegal casinos operated in full view of the police with reports claiming they were turning over nearly $200 million a year (equivalent to $1.8 billion today). The overt way in which these casinos operated, combined with little serious action being taken, led to a string of allegations that Askin was on the take. An insider of Perc Galea (p86) claimed that Askin and Police Commissioner Fred Hanson were each being paid bribes of $100,000 ($1 million today) a year.[2]

Apart from the Moffitt Royal Commission, Askin actively avoided establishing inquiries or royal commissions into police corruption and organised crime, claiming that organised crime did not exist in New South Wales.

After his death and later that of his wife, the Askin estate was valued at several million dollars, deemed to be more than could have been accrued from his government wage or known business activity. Much of it, according to the tax office, came from undisclosed sources outside of shares or gambling.[3]

In 1986 the then premier Neville Wran was asked if he thought Askin was a crook. He replied, 'Yes.'[4]

Sir Robert Askin photographed with a Liberal Party poster in Pittwater Road, Manly, 17 November 1973. © Fairfax Photos

SIR ROBERT
ASKIN

(1909–1981)

KEEP N.S.W. IN STRONG HANDS

Liberal

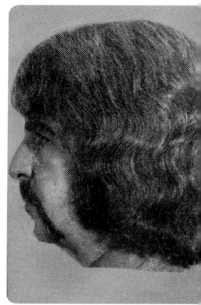

KARL
BONNETTE

(BORN 1935)

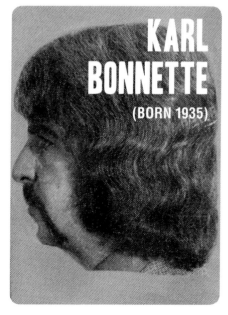

> *In underworld parlance, Karl Frederick Bonnette is a man to respect. So revered is he by lesser lights that he has earned a euphemistic title – the Godfather.*

Bob Bottom, 1979[1]

A police raid on Karl Bonnette's home in 1978 uncovered a memo in which a friend referred to him as 'The Godfather'. Bonnette claimed it was a joke on account of his age, but the name stuck: '… all of a sudden I became the Godfather, for no good reason at all. I could have been Machine Gun Kelly, but it was the Godfather.'[2]

Despite keeping a low profile and avoiding the type of publicity such people as George Freeman (p85) or Lennie McPherson (p98) received, he was often referred to as a major player in Sydney crime. In 1978 he was named in parliament by Premier Neville Wran as a leader of the Sydney underworld and in 1985 his name appeared on a National Crime Authority list of possible targets, along with Abe Saffron (p110), Robert Trimbole (p118), Stan Smith (p114) and 'Paddles' Anderson (p61).

In 1972, Bonnette allegedly hosted a group of leading criminals to 'discuss the current activities re organised crime'.[3] They were known as 'the Double Bay meetings', and among those said to be present were Smith, McPherson, Freeman, Anderson and state ALP parliamentarian Albert Sloss, MLA. Bonnette says the meetings never took place. 'Most of those people have never been in my home ever. Wherever I've lived.'[4]

Over four years in the mid-seventies, $771,416 (equal to about $3.2 million today) passed through three of his bank accounts. When questioned, he claimed not to have any financial records regarding this money as he kept them in his head. 'What I remember, I remember,' he said.[5] 'A lot more money goes through the railways and they're running at a loss, aren't they? I was too.'[6]

Mug shot of Karl Bonnette, c1975. Justice & Police Museum collection

> *If you repeat one word of what we have said here today to the Queensland police I will shoot you stone dead, and anything you say to them, naturally they will repeat back to me.*

Alleged threat made by Detective Sergeant Fred Krahe to Brifman[1]

Shirley Brifman was found dead in a Brisbane apartment shortly after giving police and the ABC damning testimonies directly naming 34 corrupt New South Wales police officers and their activities. Despite obvious motivations for her murder no inquest was held, and her death was attributed to a heart attack or self-inflicted drug overdose.

Brifman claimed she had been clearing $5000 a week (equivalent to $47,000 today) running brothels in Sydney under the protection of Detective Sergeant Fred Krahe (p97), whom she had paid more than $20,000 ($179,000) – $100 per week for four years – for the privilege.[2] She also claimed Krahe introduced her to Commissioner Norman Allan (p57) in 1969, who had told her to freely go about her business and said that anyone who harassed her would have to answer to him.[3]

Some claim Krahe was responsible for her death, travelling to Brisbane and with the aid of a Queensland colleague forcing drugs down her throat with a tube.[4] Despite looming charges based on Brifman's testimony, Krahe was allowed to retire from the police force shortly after her death, declared medically unfit. As the charges were internal, once he had retired from the force he was outside the jurisdiction of the police disciplinary board and the charges could no longer be heard.

Shirley Brifman, c1965. Anonymous source

SHIRLEY BRIFMAN

(1935–1972)

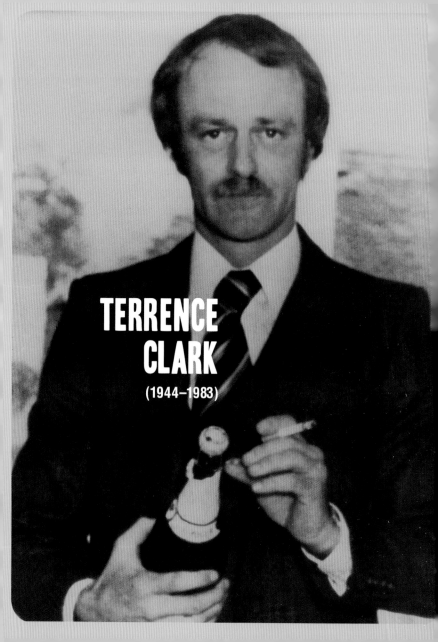

TERRENCE
CLARK
(1944–1983)

> *With Clark, though, there was an extra dimension not present in some criminals … in my book the man was wicked – evil, as were some of his cohorts.*

The Hon Donald Stewart, former judge and Royal Commissioner[1]

Described as having 'mad eyes' and being 'completely Machiavellian',[2] Terrence Clark became the head of the Mr Asia syndicate, a group responsible for importing huge quantities of heroin into Australia during the late seventies.

After serving time for stealing in his home country of New Zealand, he turned to drug dealing and began working for Christopher Martin Johnston, the original 'Mr Asia'. Clark started as a distributor in Auckland but quickly moved into importation, dealing in cannabis and later heroin. He was charged with importing heroin in 1975 but absconded while on bail, moving the following year to Sydney, where he expanded operations.

Over the next three years Clark oversaw the importation of at least 200 kilograms of 'Number One Chinese White, 85 to 93 per cent' pure heroin into Australia.[3]

Clark was thought to have been responsible for ordering or committing the murders of six syndicate members, although he was only ever convicted of one – that of Johnston, whose handless corpse was found in an abandoned British quarry in 1979. Clark received a 37-year sentence but died in Parkhurst prison on the Isle of Wight. He left an estate estimated to be worth up to $50 million (equivalent to $174 million today) to his young son.[4]

Terrence Clark, also known as Mr Asia, c1975. Anonymous source

The amount of money involved exceeds many billions of dollars and strikes right into the heart of organised crime, banks, gold mines, export fraud and institutionalised corruption.

Syndication International, 1986[1]

Bruce 'Snapper' Cornwell won his nickname from his 'supposed ability to slip through police nets'.[2] Although police believed from the 1970s that he was a major player in illegal drug importation, they were never able to prove it.

In 1984 the newly created National Crime Authority (NCA) identified Cornwell as an important target. Believing that 'ordinary police methods of investigation were unlikely to be effective'[3] against Cornwell the NCA applied for, and was granted, permission to use special coercive powers in pursuit of him. After a lengthy investigation the NCA's Operation Silo resulted in Cornwell's extradition from Britain to Australia to face 13 charges of trying to import drugs.

He was flown by helicopter from Wormwood Scrubs prison in Britain by a secret operation involving a team of 'untouchables' sent over by the Australian prime minister, Bob Hawke. He received a maximum 23-year sentence.[4]

Released in 1993, Cornwell was arrested again in 1998 for a cannabis offence resulting from a police undercover operation. His defence argued the 'sting' was so obviously phony that a man with Cornwell's experience in drug dealing would never have been deceived. 'I believe in miracles,' Cornwell commented when the jury found him not guilty.

He is currently in jail for further drug offences.

Bruce Cornwell being smuggled out of Britain into Australia. Picture taken 21 August 1986. Courtesy Fairfax Photos

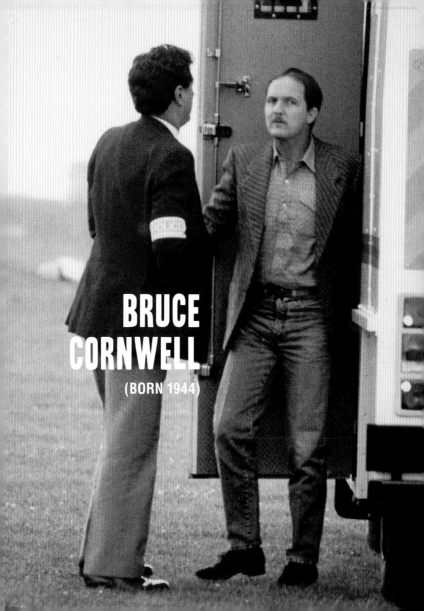

BRUCE CORNWELL

(BORN 1944)

MICHAEL
DRURY
(BORN 1953)

NEW SOUTH WALES POLICE FORCE 1972–2000

On 6 June 1984 Detective Senior Constable Michael Drury was shot twice through the kitchen window of his family home. Believing he would die, he gave a deposition outlining that on three separate occasions Detective Sergeant Roger Rogerson (p109) had offered him bribe money to go soft in his testimony against Melbourne drug dealer Alan Williams.

Williams eventually pleaded guilty to a charge of conspiring to murder Drury. He testified that he had discussed murdering Drury with Chris Flannery (p82) and Rogerson over dinner, during which the two men agreed to murder Drury for $100,000. Williams said he asked Flannery if he thought Rogerson could be trusted, to which

Flannery replied: 'Yeah, I do, but just on the off chance something happens, it won't be done unless he is with me.'[2]

Rogerson faced charges of attempting to bribe Drury and later for conspiring to murder him, but was acquitted on both counts. Drury returned to policing but retired from service in 2000, believing his career had been irreparably undermined by colleagues who could not forgive him for speaking out against another officer.[3]

A report by Chief Superintendent D W A Kelly highlighted serious shortcomings in police handling of the shooting, observing that Drury had 'to suffer the indignity of senior police not giving him the support he rightly deserved,' and that he was also the victim of a rumour campaign that claimed the shooting was 'a result of his association with a prostitute.'[4]

Detective Senior Sergeant Michael Drury receiving an award at the Police Academy in Goulburn, 22 January 1993. © Fairfax Photos

> *The first flight ... [the pilot] is only going to bring down one kilo [of heroin] ... The next one after that will be eight and the third will be forty ... After that they can jam this job up their arses and I can sit back and retire.*

Detective Sergeant Bill Duff, 1985[1]

NEW SOUTH WALES POLICE FORCE 1965–1986

In the early eighties Bill Duff was one of the state's top homicide detectives, receiving favourable press coverage for solving crimes and earning commendations for his case work from the police commissioner.[2]

But by 1985 things started changing, as his reputation morphed from that of a respected policeman to something more sinister. Duff was alleged to have approached Detective Sergeant John McNamara of the Bureau of Crime Intelligence seeking information about a criminal contact. During that conversation McNamara claimed Duff discussed a plan to import three shipments of heroin into Australia. 'Roger and I have it all worked out. If we don't do it some other c--- will'.[3]

Duff claimed he was simply involved in a seafood importing business, but with the aid of federal police phone taps he was found guilty of misconduct and dismissed from the force.

Like his friend and colleague Roger Rogerson, Duff received his first conviction in the 1990s. In 1994 he was pulled over by police who found 62 grams of heroin and more than $17,000 in cash in his car. He received a two-year sentence. In 1999 he was also charged with involvement in a lab producing methylamphetamine, but the charges were eventually dropped.[4]

Bill Duff photographed at the CIB, 28 June 1979. © Fairfax Photos

BILL DUFF

(BORN 1945)

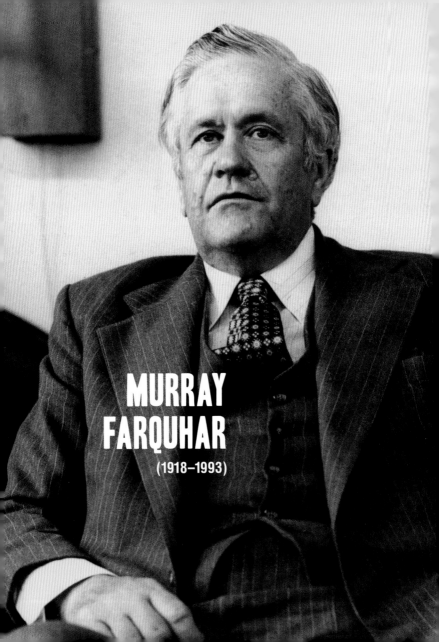

**MURRAY
FARQUHAR**

(1918–1993)

NEW SOUTH WALES CHIEF STIPENDIARY MAGISTRATE 1971–1979

In 1985 retired Chief Stipendiary Magistrate Murray Farquhar became the first former or serving member of the bench to be convicted and to serve time in a New South Wales prison.

He was found guilty of having tried to influence a fellow magistrate in 1977 to not commit Kevin Humphreys, head of the New South Wales Rugby League, for trial. Humphreys had been charged with defrauding the Balmain Leagues Club. In 1983 the ABC's *Four Corners* program alleged that the then Premier Neville Wran had asked Farquhar to go easy on Humphreys. The story sparked one of the most high-profile royal commissions in the state's history, with Wran stepping down until its findings were made public.

Headed by Sir Laurence Street, the commission cleared Wran but uncovered Farquhar's inappropriate relationships with leading criminals such as George Freeman (p85), from whom he regularly received racing tips. Street said the relationship 'showed that Mr Farquhar was indeed obligated to Mr Freeman and hence vulnerable at his hands'.[2]

Murray Farquhar in Sydney, 25 May 1979. © Fairfax Photos

You're not a protected species you know – you're not a fucking koala bear!

Alleged threat made to a New South Wales police officer by Flannery[1]

Melbourne-born contract killer and thug Christopher Dale Flannery – nicknamed 'Mr Rent-a-kill' – bulldozed his way into the Sydney underworld in the early eighties. Flannery would do anything to anybody for the right price, and his unorthodox approach took Sydney criminals by surprise.

'One day I got a tip-off that a Melbourne hitman was going around offering to kill me for $50,000. It turned out to be Chris Flannery,' Neddy Smith (p113) wrote in 1995.[2] Even George Freeman (p85) was intimidated – 'It's not something I readily admit, but Flannery scared me. Anyone who wasn't scared of him didn't know the man.'[3]

Described by police as an uncontrollable criminal and a wild-card, Flannery was alleged to have shot Constable Michael Drury (p77) in collaboration with Roger Rogerson (p109) on the orders of Melbourne drug dealer Alan Williams.[4] Lennie McPherson (p98) told police that shortly before the shooting he supplied Flannery with three guns. 'He didn't know what Flannery wanted the guns for, but after Flannery got the guns, Michael Drury was shot in the kitchen of his home over on the north side, and Flannery returned two of those guns to McPherson. And, shortly after that, Flannery disappeared.'[5]

Flannery is also alleged to have shot Anthony Eustace (Tony) Anderson during the Dale Catherine Payne inquest (p102). Eventually his erratic behaviour left him with no allies and he disappeared on 9 May 1985. Some, including ex-policeman Clive Small, believe George Freeman killed him in an effort to quell the Sydney gang wars, while others such as Neddy Smith believe police killed him.

Christopher Dale Flannery, c1984 © Fairfax Photos

CHRISTOPHER FLANNERY

(1949–1985)

GEORGE
FREEMAN
(1934–1990)

... there was only one thing I wanted out of life. I wanted to be a crook. Not just any crook, but the crook, the BIGGEST – the man with money, power, influence. Working for a living never entered my head.

George Freeman, 1988[1]

In 1977 the *National Times* published a grainy photograph (see p54) taken at Randwick Racecourse showing underworld identity George Freeman in company with New South Wales Chief Stipendiary Magistrate Murray Farquhar (p81). It became an iconic image, representing links between criminals and the state. For many it exemplified 'everything that was rotten about the state of NSW in the 1970s'.[2]

A charismatic and persuasive man, Freeman rose to become one of Sydney's leading figures of organised crime, in particular dominating the racing and illegal gambling industries. He formed strong allegiances with Lennie McPherson (p98) and Stan 'The Man' Smith (p114), with the trio allegedly controlling much of the vice trade in Sydney during the 1970s.[3]

Members of the Gaming Squad used to follow Freeman around the casinos at night as he collected money and put it in his boot. He drove at 'incredible speeds'. Members of the squad joked that 'rather than try and bash our heads up against a brick wall and have him arrested for his involvement in organised crime … we'd be better off locking him up for driving at a speed dangerous to the public, because at least we'd get a result'.[4]

Freeman always denied involvement with illegal drugs, although many of his close associates were undeniably engaged in dealing and trafficking. It is perhaps ironic, then, that his death from an asthma attack at the age of 56 was linked by the coroner to a long-standing, secret addiction to the (legal) drug pethidine.[5]

George Freeman in Sydney on 29 April 1988 after beating a Supreme Court action to prevent the publication of his autobiography. © Fairfax Photos

I couldn't go to the races and not have a bet! That would be the same as going to church and not praying.

From David Hickie, *The prince and the premier*[1]

Charming, charismatic and with friends in high places, Perc Galea was one of Sydney's biggest racetrack bettors. He also shared his tips around, making him a popular man with punters far and wide. In 1962 he gave his Melbourne Cup selection on television – 'I won't give you the winner, but I'll pick them one, two and three … Even Stevens first, Comicquita second and Aquanita third' – which was exactly how they finished.[2]

Despite many of his business interests operating outside the law, most people remember him as a colourful character rather than a criminal. However, his impact on the development of organised crime in New South Wales cannot be overstated.

He was 'the uncrowned king of illegal casinos in Sydney',[3] operating some of the most successful and lucrative gambling dens in the city. It was one of Galea's Double Bay casinos that economics lecturer Dr Geoffrey Lewis studied throughout 1974 (see p17). Staff told him the casino profited $30,000 to $60,000 a week (equivalent to $198,000–$396,000 today), from which they paid $5000 ($33,000) a week in bribes to senior police and politicians.[4]

These payments played a vital role in institutionalising corruption in Sydney. With them, bribery became an accepted tool of business, giving established criminals new avenues of access to those in power.

Despite several heart attacks, Galea continued betting against doctors' advice and died at the age of 67.

Perc Galea recovering in St Vincent's Hospital, Sydney, 28 August 1963.
© Fairfax photos

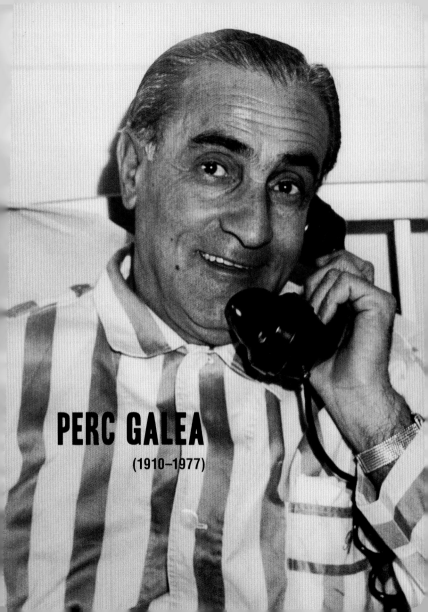

PERC GALEA

(1910–1977)

FRED HANSON

(1914–1980)

> *And I won't have big moustaches. So far as I'm concerned the hairies can shave off or ship out … I want to see trousers neatly pressed and shoes polished and shining, for I believe smartness earns respect.*

Fred Hanson's thoughts on what makes a good cop, 1972[1]

NEW SOUTH WALES POLICE COMMISSIONER 1972–1976

The fashion-conscious and controversial Frederick John 'Slippery' Hanson took over the top job when Norm Allan (p57) resigned after the Arantz scandal (p65).

According to the 1997 royal commission into the New South Wales police service, one of his first actions was to allow officers whom Shirley Brifman (p70) named as corrupt to leave the force 'hurt on duty'. As a result the serious allegations made against them were never resolved, and they left the force with full pension and leave entitlements.[2]

Like Allan and the then Premier Robert Askin (p66), Hanson was also said to be receiving massive bribes from illegal casinos in return for letting them operate. 'It is very difficult to gain entry and obtain evidence,' he pleaded in 1973.[3] This was despite the fact that journalists repeatedly entered and documented the city's casinos, and magistrates publicly stated that police had more than enough power to close them down.[4]

Among his many other questionable actions, he promoted Sergeant Jack McNeill to inspector during the Moffitt Royal Commission, in which Justice Moffitt said Sergeant McNeill and his associates were involved in a 'deliberate or corrupt' cover-up of details relevant to their investigation into organised crime in clubs.[5] He is also alleged to have gone duck shooting with Robert Trimbole (p118).[6]

Fred Hanson gives an address in Sydney, early 1970s. © Fairfax Photos

Early on the morning of 7 February 1986 the body of Sallie-Anne Huckstepp was found floating in a lake in Centennial Park. She had been brutally murdered the night before.

Like Shirley Brifman (p70) who was alleged to have been murdered 15 years earlier, Huckstepp knew a great deal about police corruption. In 1985 she appeared on national television detailing a range of corrupt practices she had encountered over a period of ten years. The move was prompted by the fatal shooting of her then boyfriend Warren Lanfranchi by Detective Sergeant Roger Rogerson (p109).

Despite a large number of suspects, a drawn-out four-year inquest failed to gather enough evidence to solve her murder. Andrew Haesler, who represented Huckstepp's family at the inquest, voiced frustrations with the lack of transparency of the inquiry: 'Inquiries weren't made. Material wasn't passed on. We were kept in the dark.'[2]

In the mid-1990s Neddy Smith (p113) was charged with but later acquitted of her murder.

Sallie-Anne Huckstepp entering the Magistrates Court in Castlereagh Street, Sydney, 19 February 1982. © Fairfax Photos

SALLIE-ANNE
HUCKSTEPP

(1954–1986)

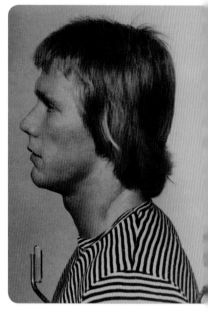

DAVID
KELLEHER
(BORN 1953)

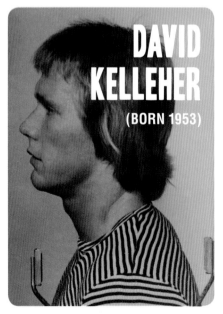

D.J. KELLEHER
15.4.53   1.80
27.1.78   2147

D.J. KELLEHER
15.4.53   1.80
27.1.78   2147

There is not going to be any brass band after I die singing 'For he's a jolly good fellow'. I am not a good person in any respect. I have been a criminal nearly all my adult life. My ethics are in the gutter.

David Kelleher, 1988[1]

Known as 'The Boss' in underworld circles, David Kelleher was sentenced to life imprisonment in 1988 for conspiring to import heroin worth $11 million (equivalent to $20 million today) into Australia.

During his trial Kelleher claimed he was involved with corrupt elements from within the New South Wales police, and offered his thoughts on the scale: 'If you think there is a can of worms being opened up in Queensland in the Fitzgerald inquiry, then you can take my word for it, you have a container-full to deal with down here.'[2]

Kelleher started his life in crime early. A drop-out from Trinity Grammar School, at the age of 18 he participated in a gang rape for which he was sentenced to ten years in jail.[3] After his release Kelleher went on to become a prolific drug dealer and an associate of Neddy Smith (p113).[4] He also attracted media attention as a boyfriend of murdered whistleblower Sallie-Anne Huckstepp (p90).

Mug shot of David Kelleher, 27 January 1978. Anonymous source

> *When he was a mere Detective Seargent he told senior officers what to do and what not to do. He was a tour de force, and he had killed people. He had murdered people.*
>
> The Hon Don Stewart[1]

NEW SOUTH WALES POLICE FORCE 1929–1966

At the retirement dinner for Detective Inspector Ray Kelly, the then premier Robert Askin (p66) said, 'no fictional detective could hold a candle to Ray Kelly'.[2] He was Sydney's most celebrated and high-profile police officer, renowned for being able to catch his man.

He had a reputation among criminals for 'verballing' (telling a court that a suspect confessed verbally to a crime) and 'fixing' (setting up) criminals. The tactics he used to force confessions were extreme. The Hon Don Stewart – former judge and royal commissioner, and first chair of the National Crime Authority – recalled as a young constable seeing Kelly hang a suspect over the balcony of the Criminal Investigation Bureau by his ankles, saying 'Confess or I'll drop you'.[3]

Kelly nurtured close relationships with criminals such as Lennie McPherson (p98). '[Kelly's] problem was that the only worthwhile informant to a detective is an active criminal – and he prided himself on his informants. Consequently he got mixed up with the real heavy criminals,' a fellow detective once told journalist David Hickie.[4] Hickie claimed that Kelly was heavily involved in running abortion rackets with Dr Reginald Stuart-Jones and his partner Richard Reilly (p105).[5]

Detective Sergeant C Behren, Detective Sergeant Ray Kelly and Detective M Wild in College Street, Sydney, date unknown. © Fairfax Photos

RAY KELLY

(1906–1977)

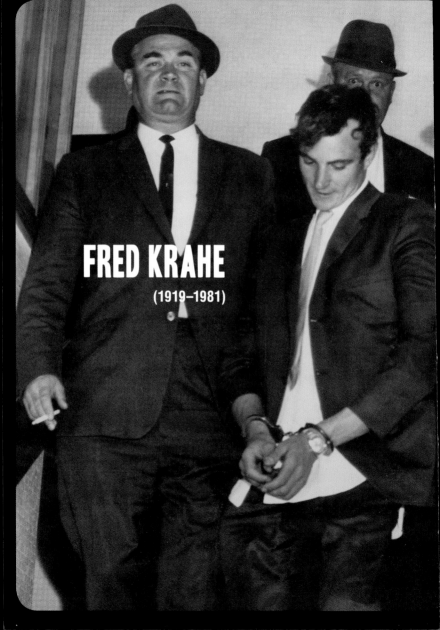

FRED KRAHE

(1919–1981)

> *Krahe had his own pricing scheme …You'd pay him to get bail … you'd pay for remands, you'd pay whether or not he gave verbal evidence against you, and you'd pay again if he decided not to give evidence against you at all.*

George Freeman, 1988[1]

NEW SOUTH WALES POLICE FORCE 1940–1972

Feared by both police and criminals alike, Detective Sergeant Fred Krahe's reputation was such that even the nastiest of thugs chose to address him as 'Mr Krahe'.

Serving alongside Ray Kelly (p94), Krahe was renowned for his criminal contacts and his ability to put crooks behind bars. During the 1966 capture of jail breakers Peter Walker and Ronald Ryan, Krahe was reported to have boldly approached the heavily armed Walker, saying 'Put your hands up or I'll blow your … head off!'[2]

Prostitute Shirley Brifman (p70) caused his downfall when she made serious allegations about Krahe's corrupt activities to police in 1971. Departmental charges were prepared, but Krahe was allowed to retire 'medically unfit' with a thrombosis of the leg before they could be laid.

After leaving the force he became a hired gun of sorts, evicting tenants for the Victoria Point developer Frank Theeman. He was also blamed for spreading false rumours about anti-drugs campaigner Donald Mackay, claiming he had run off with another woman after his disappearance.[3]

The murder of Police Superintendent Don Fergusson (whose body was found in the toilets of Police CIB headquarters, an apparent suicide) has also been attributed to him.[4]

Detective Sergeant Fred Krahe (left) escorts Peter Walker in Sydney, 5 January 1966. © Fairfax Photos

I'm the toughest man in fucking Sydney. I can kill anyone I fucking well want to, but I can't get my fucking dinner on time!

Lennie McPherson to his first wife, 1960[1]

During the 1974 Moffitt Royal Commission Lennie McPherson was described as 'a vicious, powerful criminal who is so well entrenched in organised crime activity in New South Wales that he is often referred to in the media and by his associates as "Mr Big"'.[2]

Most of his early life was spent in and out of court and prison, but by the end of the 1950s his relationship as an 'informer' for the likes of Detective Sergeant Ray Kelly (p94) saw his fortunes change. 'McPherson is the man who runs this state and has since 1957 to my knowledge', fellow criminal Neddy Smith (p113) once wrote.[3]

McPherson emerged from the gang wars of the 1960s as a dominant player along with criminals such as George Freeman (p85) and Stan Smith (p114). Together they controlled much of the vice operation in Sydney, supplying illegal gambling machines and running protection rackets.

A police visit to his Gladesville home in the eighties revealed that the precautions a crime boss must take to protect himself can affect even the simplest things in life – 'He had bulletproof glass even on his wire screen door at the front. It was wire there, but there was bulletproof glass behind it, so it really wasn't a fly screen as such.'[4]

In 1994, at the age of 73, McPherson was sentenced to a maximum four-year jail term for his role in organising the beating of a family business associate. He died in Cessnock Correctional Centre in 1996.[5]

Lennie McPherson outside his Gladesville home, 7 September 1978.
© Fairfax Photos

LENNIE MCPHERSON

(1921–1996)

JUANITA
NIELSEN

(1937–1975)

> **Mrs Nielsen says she has no time for ratbags interested in publicity or pushing some political line, but she has real concern for the little people pushed out by the developers.**
>
> *Sydney Morning Herald*, 12 October 1974

On 4 July 1975 the outspoken newspaper publisher Juanita Nielsen disappeared, sparking one of the most high-profile mysteries in Sydney's history.

Before her disappearance, her Kings Cross paper, *Now*, had been lobbying against major development in the area. Additionally her uneasy relationship with the likes of Jim Anderson (p62) and his associates helped create a long list of suspects.

In 1977 journalists Tony Reeves and Barry Ward took out a full-page advertisement in the *Sydney Morning Herald* claiming to have information relating to 'a major conspiracy apparently involving police, certain developers and others having a vested interest in the destruction of green bans and their supporters'.[1]

Despite many calls for a royal commission, an inquest was not held until 1983. As well as concluding that Nielsen was likely to be dead, it also found the initial investigation was prevented from doing its job by an 'atmosphere of corruption, real or imagined, that existed at the time'.[2]

In 2004 fresh information was provided by a witness claiming to have seen her moments before she was murdered, and in 2007 Abe Saffron's son said he had firsthand evidence regarding her fate, but to this day her case remains unsolved.

Juanita Nielsen in Potts Point, 4 October 1974. © Fairfax Photos

On 15 May 1978 the body of Dale Catherine Payne was found. The cause of death was an apparent heroin overdose. Days before, Payne had begged police to return money confiscated during a drug raid, saying, 'I have to have it tonight. It's Tony Anderson's money. If I don't give it to him tonight he'll kill me.'[2]

Narcotics Bureau agents kept this vital information from a 1978 inquest, leading coroner Len Nash to find she had died from a self-administered overdose. However, as a result of work by journalists Brian White and Steve Liebmann, new information came to light. In his 1983 report on drug trafficking, Justice Donald Stewart detailed 'direct and credible' evidence of police corruption, and suggested the government call a royal commission.[3] The government instead called a second inquest.

In 1985 the second coroner, Kevin Anderson, found the circumstance of her death suspicious, saying, 'it is likely she was murdered',[4] but due to a lack of evidence left the cause of death open.

Drug dealer Tony Anderson appeared as a witness but was murdered before the end of the second inquest, allegedly by Christopher Flannery (p82). Word at the time, according to Karl Bonnette (p69),[5] was that Anderson killed Payne.

The Narcotics Bureau agents were to be tried for perjury but the charges were dropped in 1989, the judge declaring that too much time had passed for them to receive a fair trial.[6]

102 A montage of *Sydney Morning Herald* headlines at the time of Dale Payne's death and inquests. No photos of her are known to exist.

eat threats 'known'

... "common knowledge around the ... in May 1978 that a heroin addict, Catherine Payne, claimed threats ... made to her life, a supervising ... ator of the then Federal Narcotics ... Mr Terence Alton, told Castle-... treet Court yesterday...

In answer to a further question put by Mr Porter, Mr Alton said that Dale Payne had "an undesirable relationship" and was "unduly familiar" with Mr Spencer.

Mr Alton said that $23,800 was seized when the Glenview...

expenses and also to help pay for her defence in the court case.

She allegedly told her father that she had given $3,500 of the money to a man named Brian Alexander...

Former agent began dossier after addict's death

Murder file disappears

rime authority judge acts on corrupt police

... he explained   from Tony Anderson under th ... if he didn't.

narcotics ... ... terday that he had   October 1978 found that Payne   able to ...   ... "Payne...

overnment wants new inquir to death of heroin addict

State Government made an ... ducted by a form... ... Mr

roner criticises rcotics agents Payne inquest

acted a ban on ... allegation that

following a *Sixty Minutes* gram in August 1984.

He said that most of the ... had come to light ... ..., which was condu...

Miss Payne was an informa... the Narcotics Bureau and had a number of officers that feared for her life.

But two Narcotics Bureau ...

JENNY COOKE
... the second inquest ... h of heroi ... ... ine Payne ... the Attorney ... an consider ... e narcotics ... ... harged. ... oner, Mr Kev ... "the grea ... ched itself ... ath and "it i ... red". ... urned an of ... death. ... that Dale ... at Roo ... tel, Edge ... on May I ... ... of acu

tended to show that Dale Payne was not in fear of her life while on remand in prison for several months in the time leading up to

Evidence of Payne's fear 'would have been vital'

By JENNY COOKE
Evidence of fears the heroi... ... was produced...

and it was the second that ... was ...irst

Sergeant McGoldrick said he found it "surprising" that two of the narcotics agents, Richard Spencer and Peter Marzol, had been some of the sources of an article which appeared in the *Daily Mirror* before the inquest suggesting Payne may have been murdered.

The tenor of the article had the

Perjury claims n Payne case

By JENNY COOKE   circumstances in which Rowe was   Spencer and Marzol to withhold

he a 's t-ill n of acu

10. f s o

DALE CATHERINE PAYNE
(1948–1978)

RICHARD
REILLY

(1909–1967)

> *The 'black book' found on Reilly's body must be examined by an independent tribunal. The only way justice can be done to all persons who are alleged to have been named in it is for the government to order a royal commission.*
>
> J B Renshaw, Labor Party leader[1]

Richard Reilly — Sydney's baccarat king and a criminal heavyweight with convictions going back to before World War II — was shot as he left his mistress's flat on 26 June 1967. Despite opening fire on him with various weapons, his killers were horrified when Reilly got into his Maserati as if nothing had happened. During the court case it was revealed that they left the scene bickering over whether they had actually hit him.

> Don't tell me you've missed with the double-barrelled shotgun?
>
> You do not know what this man is like. He just kept coming like a b-------- tank. I fired the shotgun at him and I know I hit him. He just kept coming, got into his car after looking right at the place where I was and just backed the car out as if nothing had happened.[2]

Reilly only made it a few hundred metres before slumping over the wheel and rolling backwards into a shop window.[3]

Following his death police found diaries in which Reilly had recorded the names of his contacts. Shortly afterwards the names of Labor politicians Norman Mannix and Albert Sloss (also said to have been at the 'Double Bay meetings' – see p69) were published by the press, but journalist David Hickie claimed the list included others such as federal Labor politicians E J Ward and James Frances Cope, and detectives Ray Kelly (p94) and Fred Krahe (p97).

Despite calls for the diaries to be independently investigated, no action was ever taken.

Richard Reilly's Maserati shortly after he was shot dead, 26 June 1967.
© Fairfax Photos

NEW SOUTH WALES POLICE FORCE 1943–1962

Murray Riley – ex-detective sergeant, dual Olympian, and winner of two Commonwealth Games gold medals[1] – was 'one of the architects of organised crime in Australia'.[2]

In 1966 Riley was sentenced to 12 months in prison in New Zealand for attempting to bribe a police officer. After being deported back to Sydney in 1967 he began his corrupt involvement with clubs such as the South Sydney Junior Rugby League Club. Poker machines were generating huge amounts of cash, and Riley and his associates quickly found ways to illegally direct money into their own pockets.

After initial exposure by the media, the Moffitt Royal Commission was established to investigate claims that organised crime had infiltrated clubs.

The final report in 1974 found Riley's activities had 'at least one important aspect in common with the US Gangster pattern'. Despite not having the authority to do so, he organised directorships and employment within clubs and 'participated in and acted in organizing the skimming by illicit means and shams, of monies from the clubs.'[3]

During the seventies he developed contacts within the American Mafia and became involved in major drug importation. He was jailed in 1978 for a failed drug shipment and on his release in 1984 took up with heroin importer Neddy Smith (p113).

In 1991 he was sentenced to five years jail in the United Kingdom for a massive attempted fraud, but escaped from custody and went to Surfers Paradise, where he is rumoured to remain.

Murray Riley having a beer on the banks of the Georges River in Sydney, a day after being released from jail, 30 May 1984. © Fairfax Photos

MURRAY RILEY

(BORN 1925)

ROGER
ROGERSON
(BORN 1941)

> *I paid Roger and his police friends millions of dollars over the years – and I used him to get what I wanted. Also, he kept me out of jail for 15 years.*

Neddy Smith, 1993[1]

NEW SOUTH WALES POLICE FORCE 1958–1986

Roger Caleb Rogerson was one of the most effective detectives on the force, with a reputation among his peers as a 'very charismatic' person and 'a brilliant detective'.[2]

However, his 'scandalous' and corrupt'[3] relationship with vicious criminal Neddy Smith (p113), who became an informer for Rogerson in the mid-seventies, ultimately led to his dismissal from the police force.

He narrowly escaped prosecution on a number of serious charges – in 1981 Smith drove Warren Lanfranchi, the boyfriend of Sallie-Anne Huckstepp (p90), to a fateful meeting with Rogerson. The state coroner found Rogerson shot Lanfranchi twice 'whilst endeavouring to make an arrest', but the jury 'declined to find that the shot was fired in self defence'.[4]

In 1988 he was charged with conspiring to murder fellow police officer Michael Drury (p77) but was acquitted. In 1990 he was found guilty of conspiring to pervert the course of justice by lying about bank accounts he held under false names. Despite several appeals, he served a three-and-a-half-year prison sentence.

Rogerson's relationship with Neddy Smith became the focus of a 1994 Independent Commission Against Corruption report that brought most of these allegations to the fore. In an interview with the Historic Houses Trust in 2009 he denied the charges laid against him.

He has toured pubs capitalising on his sordid reputation, talking about what's wrong with policing today and auctioning signed photos of himself standing over Lanfranchi's corpse.[5] In 2009 he published his first book, *The dark side*.

Roger Rogerson speaks to the media at police headquarters, 19 June 1985. © Fairfax Photos

> **Mr Saffron should be employed by the Australian Forces as a camouflage expert, sir. He's done it successfully for many many years.**
>
> Jim Anderson, 1983[1]

Abe Saffron was one of Sydney's most fascinating and successful underworld figures. He had interests in more than 100 businesses, including hotels, brothels, sly-grog outfits and illegal clubs. On his death, some estimated his fortune to be at least $100 million.[2]

He was regarded as 'one of the principal characters in organised crime in Australia'[3] but managed to avoid police attention and prosecution for most of his career. This was despite being mentioned in nearly every royal commission and inquiry into organised crime since the 1950s. Many of his activities were exposed when his business associate Jim Anderson (p62) turned on him in the early eighties and detailed Saffron's corrupt dealings. Due largely to Anderson's evidence, the National Crime Authority was able to convict Saffron of tax fraud in 1988.

Perhaps his greatest skill was his ability to influence those in a position of power. Some journalists, such as Tony Reeves, believe Saffron compiled compromising dossiers on senior people ensuring they would bend to his will.

Surveillance and illegal phone taps by New South Wales police uncovered Saffron discussing how he would entertain Police Commissioner Merv Wood and the heads of 21 Division and the CIB on Friday afternoons at his office, known as Lodge 44.[4]

Saffron aggressively defended his name, and won many defamation lawsuits, particularly about being called Mr Sin. In 2005 he won a defamation suit against the authors of a crossword who listed 'Abe Saffron' as the answer to the question, 'Who is the Sydney underworld figure nicknamed Mr Sin?'[5]

Abe Saffron at his Roosevelt Club in Sydney, January 1951.
© Fairfax Photos

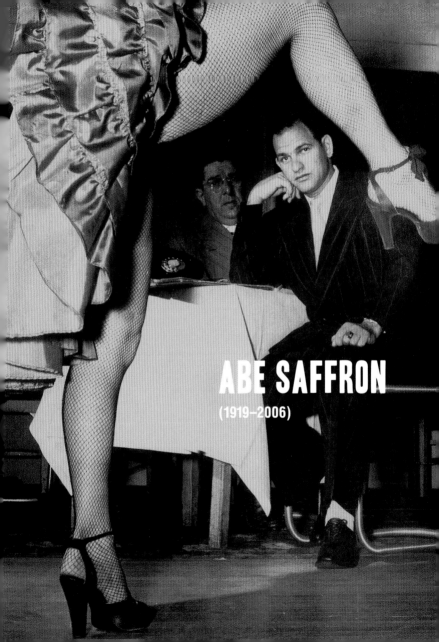

ABE SAFFRON

(1919–2006)

NEDDY SMITH

(BORN 1944)

A.S.SMITH

27·11·44

1.9

11·8·76

110

Arthur Stanley 'Neddy' Smith – convicted murderer, rapist and armed robber – has said he could do whatever he wanted during the 1980s. He'd been welcomed into the 'barbeque set', a 'clique of senior and/or corrupt police in the 1980s who regularly socialised together'.[2]

In his 1993 autobiography Smith described how police had given him the 'green light' to commit any crime he pleased, providing he didn't kill any cops. 'I had police organising crimes for me to do, then keeping me informed as to how much – if any – progress was being made in the investigations.'[3]

In the early nineties the Independent Commission Against Corruption substantiated many of his claims. In his 1994 report on police–criminal relationships, Commissioner Ian Temby QC said, 'I conclude that over a period in excess of a decade Smith was helped by various police officers, who provided him with information, looked after him when charges were laid or threatened, and generally acted in contravention of their sworn duty.'[4]

He is currently serving two life sentences for murder in the hospital of Long Bay Correctional Complex; he has advanced Parkinson's disease. In 2008 a spokesman for the New South Wales Attorney General's office said, 'We intend to keep Mr Smith behind bars for the rest of his life.'[5]

Mug shot of Arthur 'Neddy' Smith, 11 August 1976. Anonymous source

Look, he's a politician … You know, as well as I do, they're the shiftiest bunch of fucking people that ever, ever lived.

Stan Smith on Neville Wran's intentions to legalise casinos, 1976[1]

In 1978 the then premier Neville Wran named Stanley John 'Stan the Man' Smith as a leading figure of the Sydney underworld.

Smith started carving out a name for himself in the late fifties and over the following 20 years earned a reputation as a serious and dangerous criminal. During a consorting case in 1968 police described Smith as 'a standover criminal and international shop thief'.[2]

Smith and his criminal associates – who included George Freeman (p85) and Lennie McPherson (p98) – were alleged to have taken control of or to have a stake in virtually all underworld activity from the late sixties. On a recording Smith made in 1976, he could be heard saying, 'We run it because we put the right men, the right business administrators in

to fucking handle it, with our brain power behind it and so on.' Smith recorded the tape so it could be played to a group of illegal casino owners over lunch.[3] When it was returned to him, he was observed by police pulling the tape from the cassette and dropping it into a bin, after which they recovered it.

Freeman and Smith travelled to the United States in 1968 to develop contacts with their American counterparts. They spent six weeks as a guest of American criminal heavyweight Joseph Testa (p117).

During the Woodward Royal Commission Smith was described as 'a notorious criminal with a long history of criminal convictions and a conviction for drug trafficking on a major occasion'.[4]

Lennie McPherson (left) and Stan Smith departing Sydney on a cruise to Japan via Hong Kong, 10 July 1966. © Fairfax Photos

STAN SMITH

(1937–2010)

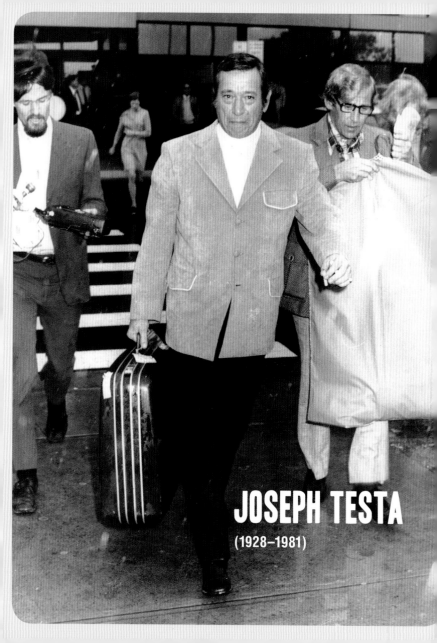

JOSEPH TESTA

(1928–1981)

Described by the FBI as a 'member of the Organised Criminal Element in Chicago, Illinois',[2] Joseph Testa developed close links with the Sydney underworld, in particular George Freeman (p85), Stan Smith (p114) and Lennie McPherson (p98).

Testa travelled to Sydney four times between 1965 and 1973, allegedly to investigate business opportunities for the Mafia. He stayed with Freeman on several of these visits and McPherson chartered an aircraft to take him pig hunting near Bourke. While in Sydney he bought a racehorse, entered into business with Freeman and denied being a 'psychopathic killer' in front of the Moffitt Royal Commission.

He also played host to his Australian friends when they went to the United States. Smith and Freeman spent six weeks with him in 1968 when they travelled to the US using false passports and in 1970 he hosted McPherson on an all-expenses-paid trip to Chicago and Las Vegas.

Testa eventually fell out with his American contacts. His house was bombed in 1977 and four years later he was killed by a car bomb.

Joseph Testa arriving at Sydney Airport, 27 November 1973.
© Fairfax Photos

> *The Trimbole story remains one of the most shameful cases in Australian law enforcement. It involves cover-ups, lies, bungles and incompetence.*
>
> John Silvester and Andrew Rule, 2002[1]

Robert 'Aussie Bob' Trimbole was one of Australia's most renowned drug dealers and criminals. He was the 'practical head' – though never an initiated member – of the Calabrian mafia, an organisation known as the 'Ndrangheta, or honoured society.[2]

Based in the horticultural town of Griffith, Trimbole started cultivating major marijuana crops in the early seventies. The profits were enormous. He invested money in legitimate businesses as a front, and expanded his empire by focusing on distribution networks. This led him into moving heroin and his strong association with the Mr Asia syndicate. By 1979 he was reportedly prepared to offer Terrence Clark (p73) $30 million (equivalent to $115 million today) to take it over.[3]

In 1977 he orchestrated the murder of Griffith businessman Donald Mackay, who had been informing police on the locations of marijuana crops,[4] and in 1979 he arranged the murders of drug couriers Isabel and Douglas Wilson for Terrence Clark.[5]

He fled Australia in 1981, and while several attempts were made to have him sent home they all failed. After he was captured in Ireland in 1984 a Dublin court decided to release him rather than send him back.

He continued to evade authorities until his death in Spain in 1987.

Robert Trimbole being escorted to the Supreme Court in Dublin, Ireland, 27 October 1984. Courtesy Fairfax Photos

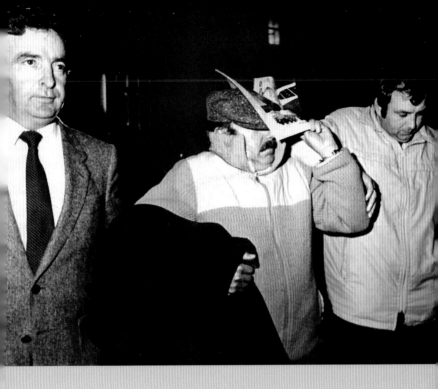

ROBERT
TRIMBOLE

(1931–1987)

NOTES

Norm Allan p57

1 David Hickie, *The prince and the premier*, Angus & Robertson, Sydney, 1985, p59.

2 Royal Commission into the New South Wales Police Service, *Final report, Volume 1: Corruption*, New South Wales Government, 1997, p48.

3 ibid.

Bill Allen p58

1 *Sydney Morning Herald*, 22 April 1982.

2 ibid.

3 Royal Commission into the New South Wales Police Service, *Final Report, Volume 1: Corruption*, New South Wales Government, 1997, p57.

4 *Sydney Morning Herald*, 22 April 1982.

5 *Sydney Morning Herald*, 16 January 1985.

Frederick 'Paddles' Anderson p61

1 *Sydney Morning Herald*, 2 February 1985.

2 ibid.

3 *Sydney Morning Herald*, 30 December 1990.

4 Interview with the Historic Houses Trust, 2009.

Jim Anderson p62

1 Interview with the Historic Houses Trust, 2009.

2 *Sydney Morning Herald*, 4 October 1983.

Philip Arantz p65

1 *Sydney Morning Herald*, 21 January 1972.

2 *Sydney Morning Herald*, 11 October 1988.

3 *Sydney Morning Herald*, 10 December 1971.

4 *Sydney Morning Herald*, 9 December 1971.

5 *Sydney Morning Herald*, 22 December 1989.

Sir Robert Askin p66

1 Stuart Littlemore, *The media and me*, ABC Books, Sydney, 1996, p115.

2 David Hickie, *The prince and the premier*, Angus & Robertson, Sydney, 1985, p59.

3 Evan Whitton, *Can of worms II*, Fairfax Library, Sydney, 2nd edition, 1987, p124.

4 ibid, p371.

Karl Bonnette p69

1 Bob Bottom, *The Godfather in Australia*, Reed, Sydney, 1979, p130.

2 Interview with the Historic Houses Trust, 2009.

3 Hon Justice Athol Moffitt, Royal commission into allegations of organised crime in clubs, *Report*, Government of New South Wales, 1974, p81.

4 Interview with the Historic Houses Trust, 2009.

5 Bob Bottom, *The Godfather in Australia*, Reed, Sydney, 1979, p131.

6 Interview with the Historic Houses Trust, 2009.

Shirley Brifman p70

1 Testimony given to Queensland police on 28 September 1971.

2 David Hickie, *The prince and the premier*, Angus & Robertson, Sydney, 1985, pp280–89.

3 *Sydney Morning Herald*, 23 September 1985.

4 David Hickie, *The prince and the premier*, Angus & Robertson, Sydney, 1985, p284.

Terrence Clark p73

1 Don Stewart, *Recollections of an unreasonable man*, ABC Books, Sydney, 2007, p145.

2 ibid and p147.

3 Richard Hall, *Greed*, Pan Books, Sydney, 1981, p43.

4 Clive Small and Tom Gilling, *Smack express*, Allen & Unwin, Sydney, 2009, pp17–18.

Bruce Cornwell p74

1 Fairfax archive.

2 *Sydney Morning Herald*, 14 December 1987.

3 *Sydney Morning Herald*, 19 December 1987.

4 *Sydney Morning Herald*, 4 and 19 December 1987.

Michael Drury p77

1 *Four Corners*, ABC Television, 14 June 2004.

2 Clive Small and Tom Gilling, *Smack express*, Allen & Unwin, Sydney, 2009, p76.

3 *Sydney Morning Herald*, 30 July 2001.

4 H F Purnell, Annexure N p12, 'In the matter of an inquiry into the investigation by the NSW Police of circumstances surrounding the shooting of M P Drury 6.6.1984: advice', 1990.

Bill Duff p78

1 Clive Small and Tom Gilling, *Smack express*, Allen & Unwin, Sydney, 2009, p123.

2 *Sydney Morning Herald*, 3 September 1981.

3 *Sydney Morning Herald*, 1 December 1985.

4 *Sydney Morning Herald*, 15 January 1994; *Smack express*, Allen & Unwin, Sydney, 2009, p134.

Murray Farquhar p81

1 *George Freeman, an autobiography*, George Freeman, Sydney, 1998, p167.

2 *Sydney Morning Herald*, 2 August 1983.

Christopher Flannery p82

1 Neddy Smith, *Catch and kill your own*, Smith Family Trust, Sydney, 1995, p169.

2 ibid, p168.

3 *George Freeman, an autobiography*, George Freeman, Sydney, 1998, p183.

4 Clive Small and Tom Gilling, *Smack express*, Allen & Unwin, Sydney, 2009, p76.

5 Former Bureau of Crime Intelligence member and assistant police commissioner Geoff Schuberg in an interview with the Historic Houses Trust, 2009.

George Freeman p85

1 *George Freeman, an autobiography*, George Freeman, Sydney, 1998, p27.

2 *Sydney Morning Herald*, 13 June 2002.

3 Clive Small and Tom Gilling, *Smack express*, Allen & Unwin, Sydney, 2009, pp33–40.

4 Former Bureau of Crime Intelligence member and assistant police commissioner Geoff Schuberg in an interview with the Historic Houses Trust, 2009.

5 *Sydney Morning Herald*, 3 August 1991.

Perc Galea p86

1 Angus & Robertson, Sydney, 1985, p45.

2 ibid, p37.

3 ibid, p20.

4 Alfred McCoy, *Drug traffic: narcotics and organized crime in Australia*, Harper & Row, Sydney, 1980, p202.

Fred Hanson p89

1 David Hickie, *The prince and the premier*, Angus & Robertson, Sydney, 1985, p276.

2 The Hon Justice J R T Wood, Royal Commission into the New South Wales police service, New South Wales Government, 1997, p48.

3 David Hickie, *The prince and the premier*, Angus & Robertson, Sydney, 1985, p277.

4 ibid.

5 *Sydney Morning Herald*, 17 October 1984.

6 *Research report on trends in police corruption*, Police Integrity Commission, Sydney, 2002, p27.

Sallie-Anne Huckstepp p90

1 John Dale, *Huckstepp: a dangerous life*, Allen & Unwin, Sydney, 2000, p28.

2 ibid, p165.

David Kelleher p93

1 *Sydney Morning Herald*, 21 September 1988.

2 ibid.

3 *Sydney Morning Herald*, 7 November 1974; *Sydney Morning Herald*, 30 October 1973.

4 *Sydney Morning Herald*, 5 February 2005; Bob Bottom, *Sydney Morning Herald*, 21 September 1988.

Ray Kelly p94

1 Historic Houses Trust interview with the Hon Don Stewart, 2008.

2 David Hickie, *The prince and the premier*, Angus & Robertson, Sydney, 1985, p300.

3 Historic Houses Trust interview with the Hon Don Stewart, 2008.

4 David Hickie, *The prince and the premier*, Angus & Robertson, Sydney, 1985, p292.

5 ibid.

Fred Krahe p97

1 *George Freeman, an autobiography*, George Freeman, Sydney, 1998, p139.

2 *Sun-Herald*, 13 December 1981.

3 Evan Whitton, *Can of worms II*, Fairfax Library, Sydney, 2nd ed, 1987, p17.

4 Tony Reeves claims in his book *Mr Big* (Allen & Unwin, Sydney, 2005, p50) that Lennie McPherson referred to Krahe as 'the person who killed Don Fergusson at the CIB' in an interview with federal police. The Hon Don Stewart also made this claim in a 2008 interview with the Historic Houses Trust: 'I can't prove this, and I didn't have the powers to investigate it at the time but I believe Krahe shot him.'

Lennie McPherson p98

1 Tony Reeves, *Mr Big*, Allen & Unwin, Sydney, 2005, p72.

2 David Hickie, *The Prince and the premier*, Angus & Robertson, Sydney, 1985, p244.

3 Neddy Smith, *Catch and kill your own*, Pan Macmillan Australia, Sydney, 1995, p9.

4 Former Bureau of Crime Intelligence member and assistant police commissioner Geoff Schuberg in an interview with the Historic Houses Trust, 2009.

5 Tony Reeves, *Mr Big*, Allen & Unwin, Sydney, 2005, pp257–62.

Juanita Nielsen p101

1 *Sydney Morning Herald*, 2 July 1977.

2 Coroner's Office, Inquest into the disappearance of Juanita Nielsen, 1983, p2.

Dale Catherine Payne p102

1 *Sydney Morning Herald*, 12 January 1985.

2 *Sydney Morning Herald*, 4 April 1985.

3 *Sydney Morning Herald*, 18 December 1984.

4 *Sydney Morning Herald*, 6 July 1985.

5 Interview with the Historic Houses Trust, 2009.

6 *Sydney Morning Herald*, 10 March 1989.

Richard Reilly p105

1 *Sydney Morning Herald*, 13 July 1967.

2 *Sydney Morning Herald*, 11 May 1968.

3 *Sydney Morning Herald*, 11 May 1968.

Murray Riley p106

1 Riley's former rowing partner, Merv Wood, went on to become New South Wales Police Commissioner and was himself the subject of corruption allegations.

2 Clive Small and Tom Gilling, *Smack express*, Allen & Unwin, Sydney, 2009, p41.

3 The Hon Atholl Moffitt, *Report,* Royal Commission, Allegations of organised crime in clubs, Government Printer, Sydney, 1974, p74.

Roger Rogerson p109

1 Neddy Smith with Tom Noble, *Neddy*, Noble House Enterprises, Prahran, 2002, p123.

2 Investigation into the relationship between Police and Criminals: *First report*, Independent Commission Against Corruption, Sydney, 1994, p24.

3 ibid, p 30.

4 The Hon Justice J R T Wood, *Report*, Royal Commission into the New South Wales Police Service, New South Wales Government, 1997, p58

5 *Sydney Morning Herald*, 22 November 2003.

Abe Saffron p110

1 Juanita Nielsen inquest, New South Wales Coroners Court, 1983, p3315.

2 *The Australian*, 16 September 2006.

3 South Australian Hansard, 9 March 1978.

4 Historic Houses Trust interview with an anonymous former detective, 2009.

5 *Sydney Morning Herald*, 28 July 2005.

Neddy Smith p113

1 Neddy Smith with Tom Noble, *Neddy*, Noble House Enterprises, Melbourne, 2002, p11.

2 The Hon Justice J R T Wood, Royal Commission into the New South Wales Police service, *Final report, Volume 1: Corruption*, Government of New South Wales, 1997, pxi.

3 Neddy Smith with Tom Noble, *Neddy*, Noble House Enterprises, Melbourne, 2002, p11.

4 Investigation into the relationship between Police and Criminals: *First Report*, Independent Commission Against Corruption, Sydney, 1994, p190.

5 *Sydney Morning Herald*, 11 December 2008.

Stan Smith p114

1 Bob Bottom, *The Godfather in Australia*, Reed, 1979, p109.

2 *Sydney Morning Herald*, 13 December 1968.

3 Bob Bottom, *The Godfather in Australia*, Reed, 1979, p110–11.

4 Bob Bottom, *The Godfather in Australia*, Reed, 1979, p122.

Joseph Testa p117

1 *Sydney Morning Herald*, 17 April 1979.

2 Clive Small and Tom Gilling, *Smack express*, Allen & Unwin, Sydney, 2009, p36.

Robert Trimbole p118

1 John Silvester and Andrew Rule, *Tough*, Floradale Productions & Sly Ink, Sydney, 2002, p157.

2 Clive Small and Tom Gilling, *Smack express*, Allen & Unwin, Sydney, 2009, p4.

3 Keith Moor, *Crims in grass castles*, Pascoe Publishing Pty Ltd, Apollo Bay, 1989, p42.

4 Clive Small and Tom Gilling, *Smack express*, Allen & Unwin, Sydney, 2009, p6.

5 ibid, p17.

ACKNOWLEDGMENTS

The author and publisher would like to thank the following individuals and organisations for their generosity and support:

Wendy Bacon, Helen Barrow, Karl Bonnette, Amelia Bowen, Caroline Butler-Bowdon, Elizabeth Burton, Nerida Campbell, Rhonda Campbell, Amy Caulfield, Dr David Clune, Rabbi Dr Jeffrey Cohen, Peter Cox, Simon Drake, Michael Drury, Jacinta Dunn, Manuela Furci, Wendy Gallagher, Gavin Harris, Matthew Holle, Sasha Huckstepp, Dr Karl James, Tina Koutsogiannis, the Hon Michael Kirby, Margaret Malone, Sir Wayne Martin, Robert McFarlane, Fiona Morris, Jules Munro, Kerry Oldfield Ellis, Charles Pickett, Hugh Piper, Tony Reeves, Roger Rogerson, Geoff Schuberg, Prof G Campbell Sharman, Clive Small, Wesley Stacey, the Hon Don Stewart, Julie Tilley, Barry Ward, Paul Warren, Peter Watts, Paul West, Evan Whitton, Marian Wilkinson and Caleb Williams.

Special thanks to Bob Bottom for advice and feedback on the content of the book, and to Caroline Mackaness for her crucial role and support in establishing this project.

Thanks also to the journalists and authors whose work was instrumental to the research for this book; to the families and friends of some of the people profiled, who did not wish to be named, but whose assistance was appreciated; and to Catherine Reade and Aimee Majurinen from Fairfax Photos.

Thank you to Simpsons Solicitors for their legal advice in relation to this publication. www.simpsons.com.au

Sponsor

INDEX

The main entry for each profiled person is indicated in **bold** type.

Published by the Historic Houses Trust
of New South Wales
The Mint, 10 Macquarie Street,
Sydney NSW 2000, Australia
www.hht.net.au

© 2010 Historic Houses Trust of New South Wales

Published in association with the exhibition *Sin city:
crime and corruption in 20th-century Sydney*,
curated by Tim Girling-Butcher, Justice & Police
Museum, Sydney, 1 May 2010–22 May 2011

Head, Exhibitions and Publications: Susan Sedgwick
Editor: Janine Flew
Designer: Beau Vandenberg
Picture rights and permissions: Alice Livingstone
Curatorial research and contributing writer: Rebecca Perrin
Pre-press: Spitting Image, Sydney
Printer: Print Plus, China

National Library of Australia
Cataloguing-in-Publication entry
Author: Girling-Butcher, Tim
Title: Sin city : crime and corruption in 20th-century
Sydney / Tim Girling-Butcher.
Edition: 1st ed.
ISBN: 9781876991364 (hbk)
Notes: Includes index.
Subjects: Organised crime – New South Wales –
Sydney – 20th century. Police corruption –
New South Wales – Sydney – 20th century. Courts –
Officials and employees – New South Wales
– Sydney – 20th century. Crime – New South Wales –
Sydney – 20th century.

Other authors/contributors: Historic Houses Trust
of New South Wales.

Dewey number: 364.106099441

Front cover: Go-go dancer, Kings Cross, c1965.
© Robert McFarlane
Back cover (top) and pp126–27: Lennie McPherson,
Chicago identity Nick Giordano and Joseph Testa on a
pig-hunting trip near Bourke, date unknown. Courtesy
Fairfax Photos; **(bottom)** Sir Wayne Martin at the Pink
Pussycat Club, Kings Cross, 1970–71. © Rennie Ellis
Photographic Archive
Page 1: $613,000 (equivalent to $1.3 million today)
confiscated by police during a drug raid, 12 May 1989.
Page 2: 'Goldie' selling *Censor* magazine, Darlinghurst
Road, Kings Cross, 1965. © Robert McFarlane
Endpapers: William Street in the rain (detail), 1967.
Reproduced from an original negative in the David Mist
photography archive, Powerhouse Museum collection.
© David Mist